AF345415

translated from life

nero suno

CONTENTS

He

I

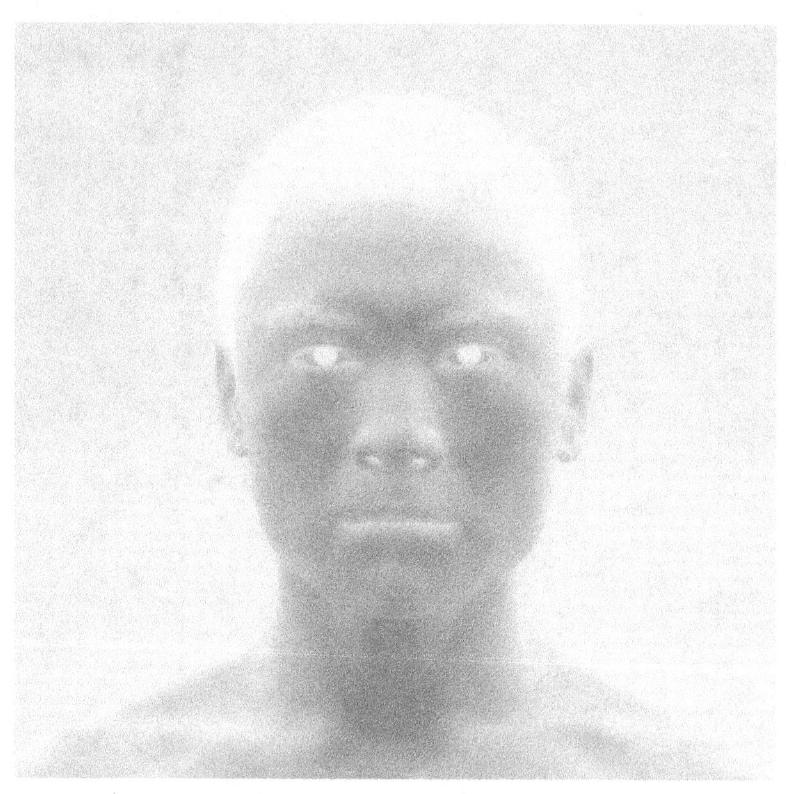

I

I grow old, I grow old,
but I am not yet old,
shining brighter than gold,
or so I should suppose...

I fear death, I fear death,
and I fear life no less.
Thanks to my consciousness,
I hold dear every breath...

I have dreams, I have dreams
that sleep in a sunbeam.
Wake me up from what seems
not my low self esteem...

I want love, I want love,
I want more than sweet love.
Proffer me a white dove:
War I can be free of.

A meaning

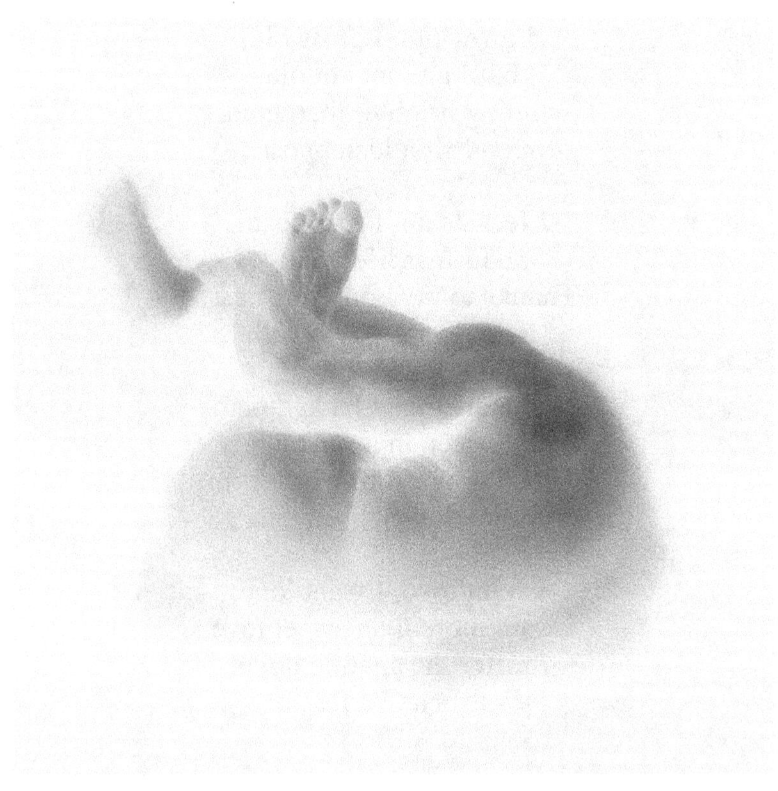

A meaning

A meaning
        forced into any kind of
feeling
      finds life worth losing in itself
as long as life is worth living to die.

Death is a meaning which fears everything
that cannot better breathe than imagine.

All feelings
          are forced out of all meanings.

Love is a meaning which means everything
howbeit truth becomes what it desires.

I am pregnant

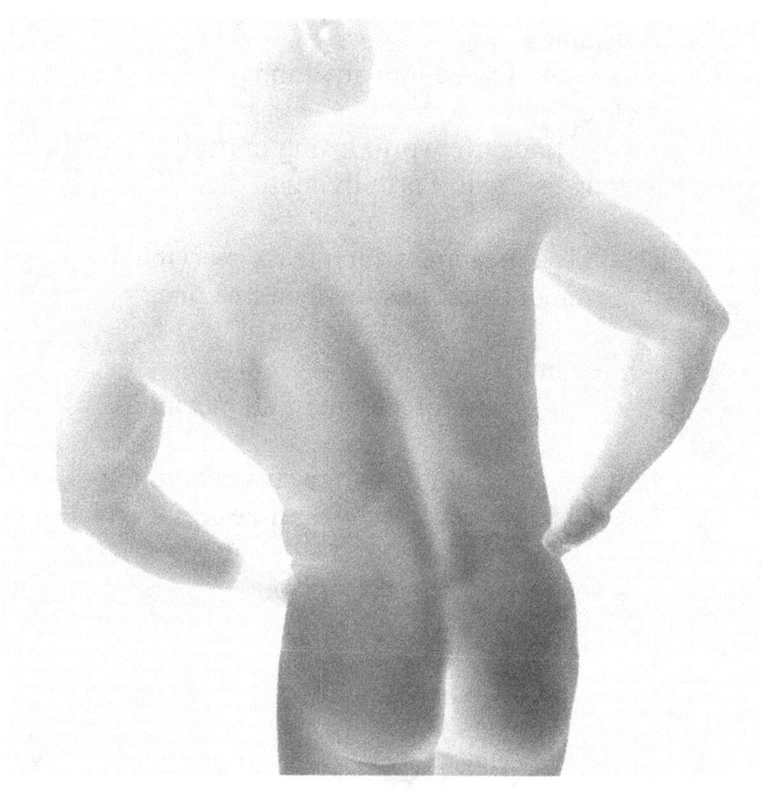

I am pregnant

I am pregnant
            with the impatience of everyday
seeming and becoming
            (spiritually).

It was created
            amidst the flowing immediacy
around the dying hesitancy
            (timely).

The infertility of
            oldness, sameness and commonness
grows impotent in its own hopelessness
            (selflessly).

In my hand opens infinity
            (wholly)
and love awakes in my mind
            (truly).

I am a genius

I am a genius

I am a genius when the whole world
sleeps in its bed of nonsense.

                              This world
makes enough sense to an idiot
sleepily awake from birth to death.

I am an idiot, too, of course,
(trying my best and worst more or less)
between the first and the last genius
who does not try when no questions yes.

Yes answers no if the sun bethinks
itself of the moon in all seasons.
Unendingly, the sky is too big
for every thought to find a reason.

I am a genius when half the world
dreams at night and half the world daydreams.

I'll never awake enough dreams

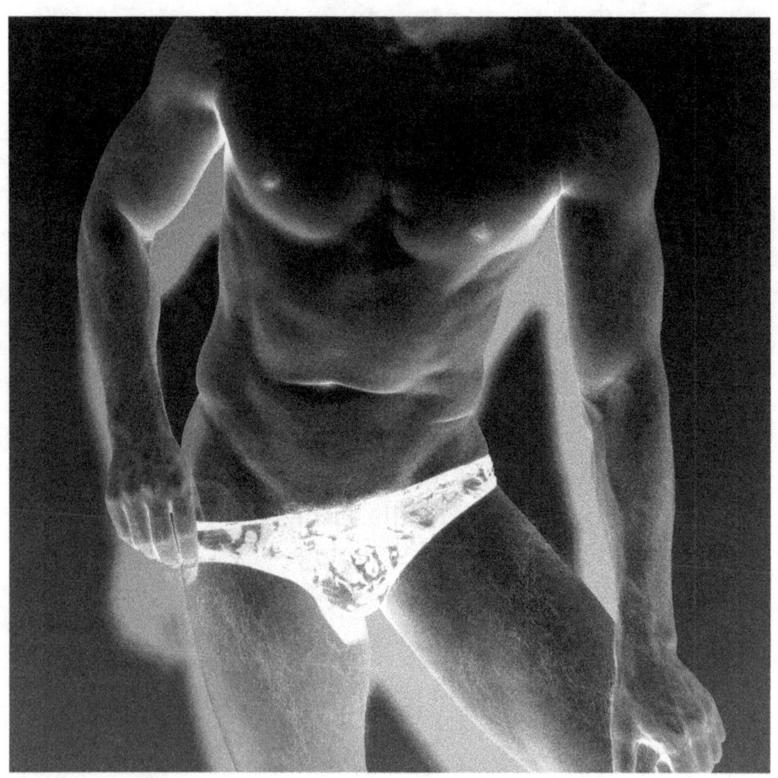

I'll never awake enough dreams

I'll never awake enough dreams to live on,
in case to live on isn't merely to dream on.
To dream on isn't merely from dusk till dawn.

I'll never lose myself in loving to hate,
for whenever I understand, it's too late.
Whenever I misunderstand, my fate.

I enslave the genius cursing inside me,
though the idiot in me hungers for me.
The hunger I feed, the demon in me.

I chase after the road to heaven and hell,
until death celebrates its very last bell.
Life celebrates, not awaiting farewell.

My self portrait

My self portrait

My self portrait contemplates a boy
(lost and found in everyday doing
and undoing) who is young enough
for the sea where an old man still dreams.

Its artistry understands the world
(in full happiness and misery)
whose good and evil show everyone's
true colors shown in a gallery.

Unlike Dorian, I shall fade in
perfect black and white so perfectly
that like Nero, I shall forever
remember to be a masterpiece.

Happiness has arrived

Happiness has arrived

Happiness has arrived,
but I don't know what to do with it,
or where to put it.

I must decide quickly,
because it won't stay here forever.
I had a plan in my head and a place in my heart,
but losing myself through the years,
I lost them both.

I must decide now,
because, once gone, it may never return.
It needs to visit others who've been waiting and crying,
and there're so many of them, waiting and crying.

I've been waiting and crying all my life,
until happiness arrived finally,
but I don't know what to do with it,
or where to put it.

With everybody getting younger

With everybody getting younger,
life tries to be what life hopes to be
for everybody.
          Life tries to find
something else to hope for rather than
hopes, perfection and true love as such.

Life tries and tries till finally fails.

Life has been and will ever be life
while doing exactly the same thing,
with nobody fearing time or death.

You don't need to understand life, baby

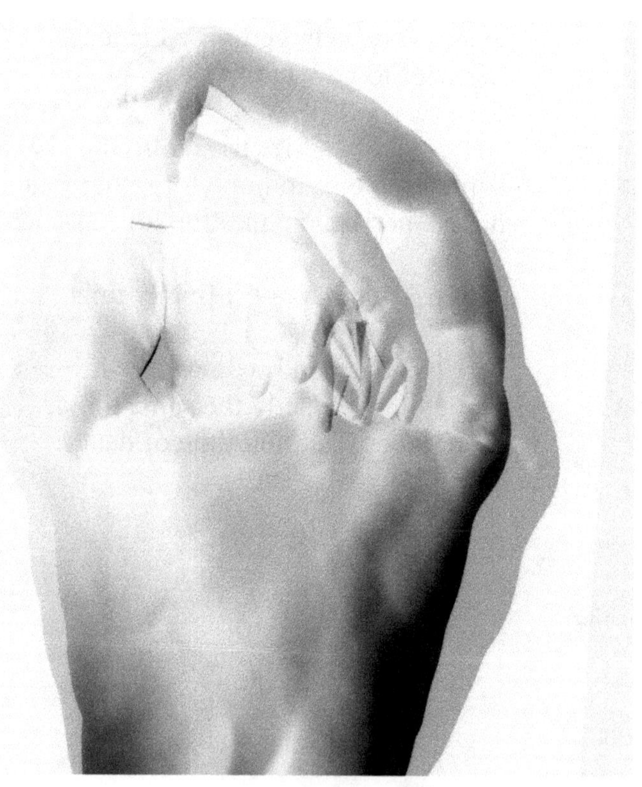

You don't need to understand life, baby,
as long as no one understands death.

As soon as no one misunderstands love,
you won't misunderstand anything.

However,

if you have to try to understand life,
you have to try to understand yourself.

And while everyone's trying hard enough,
death is as misunderstood as love.

Life is

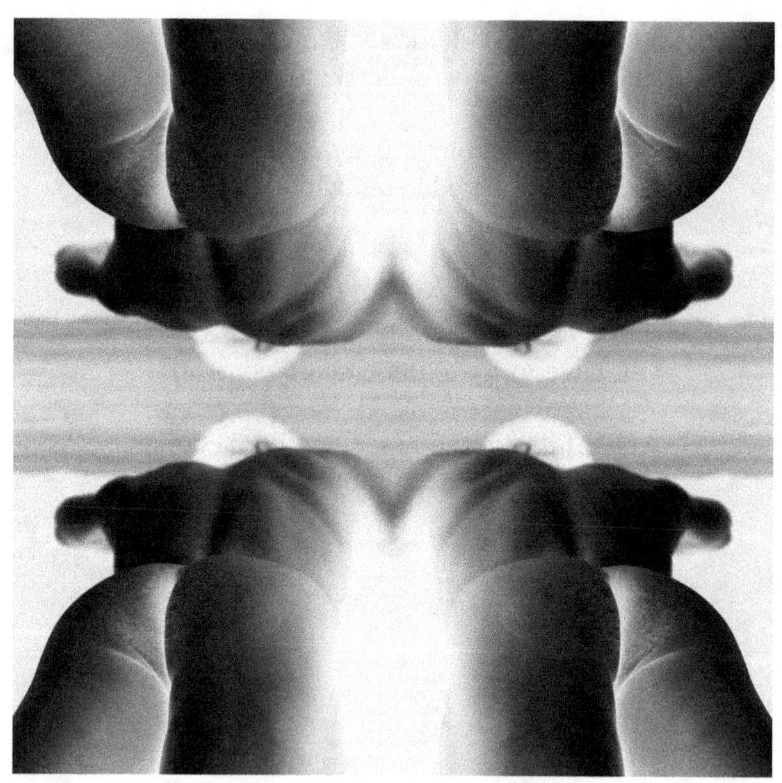

Life is

Life is long enough to get old,
short enough to forget itself
and everything in.
                 Enough! Life,
neither long nor short,
                     remembers
how to live best before die worst.
A tree (re)turns into a leaf.

Lost between yes and no, maybe
found beyond here and now, life is
both lost and found all alone.
                       Why
despite why, are we together?
Because
        despite because, life is
not to be questioned or answered.

20

Forever?

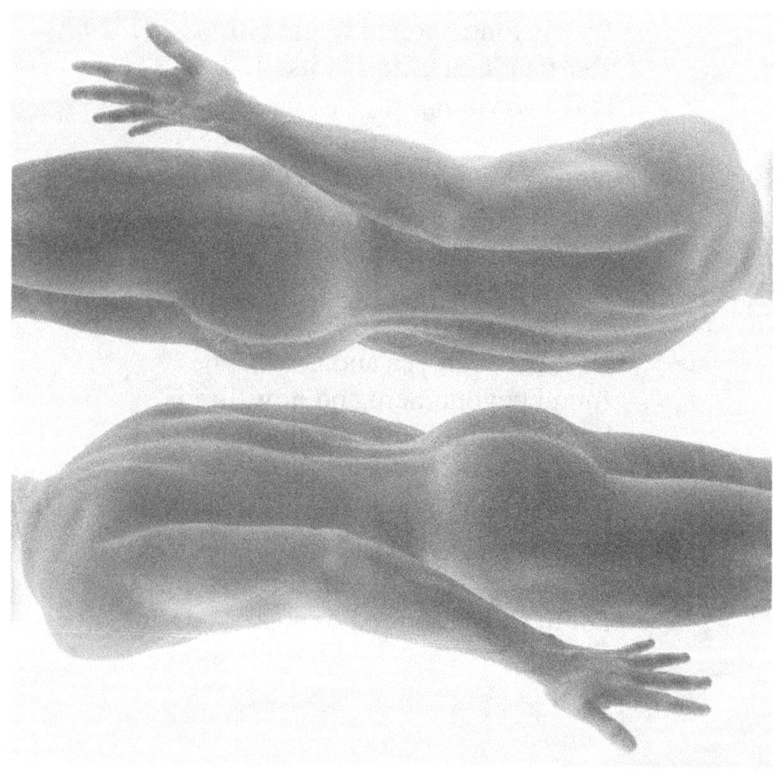

21

Forever?

Does forever awake a kiss or kill a death?
Does forever string the light beams to bend?
Is forever in a hope, if not,
does it remember, then?
Does forever contain the universal destiny of men?

Can waiting be forever,
if the awaited never come?
Can loving be forever,
even after the love is done?
Can anything be forever,
does everything turn to dust?
Can time be forever,
when time is outrun?

Is forever a question that is answered
or an answer questioned in return?
Is forever in the water that flows
or in the fire that burns?
For what reason is ever?
Forever and for ever, is ever a difference?
Forever and never, who is longer?
Forever and a day, does it sound absurd?
Does forever prove itself in a split second?
Does forever survive outside the earth?

Does forever dawn minute by minute with tomorrow?
Does forever outlive the life span of my soul?
Does forever fill up the black hole?
Does forever decide between yes and no?

If love is

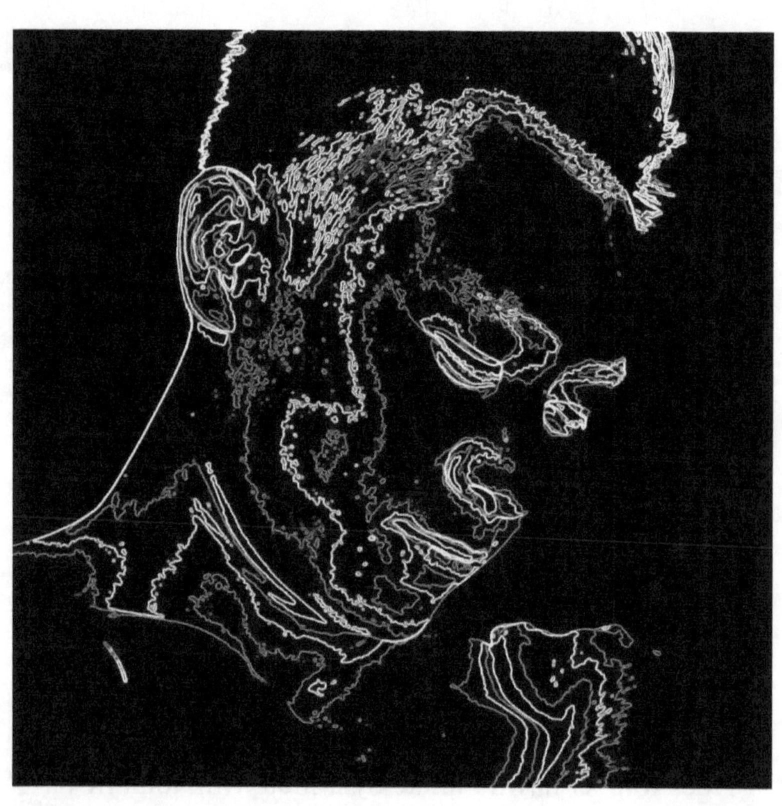

If love is

I shan't fall in love with someone
who knows exactly what love is.

If love is happiness,
the whole world has to cry for itself.
If love is sex,
romance seems romantic.
If love is beauty,
art is worthless.
If love is perfection,
hate isn't imperfection.
If love is luck,
a dream keeps on dreaming.
If love is hope,
time awaits forevermore.
If love is truth,
life is too good to be true.
If love is everything,
nothing is love.

I shall fall in love with someone
who knows love as much as (s)he could.

I endure myself

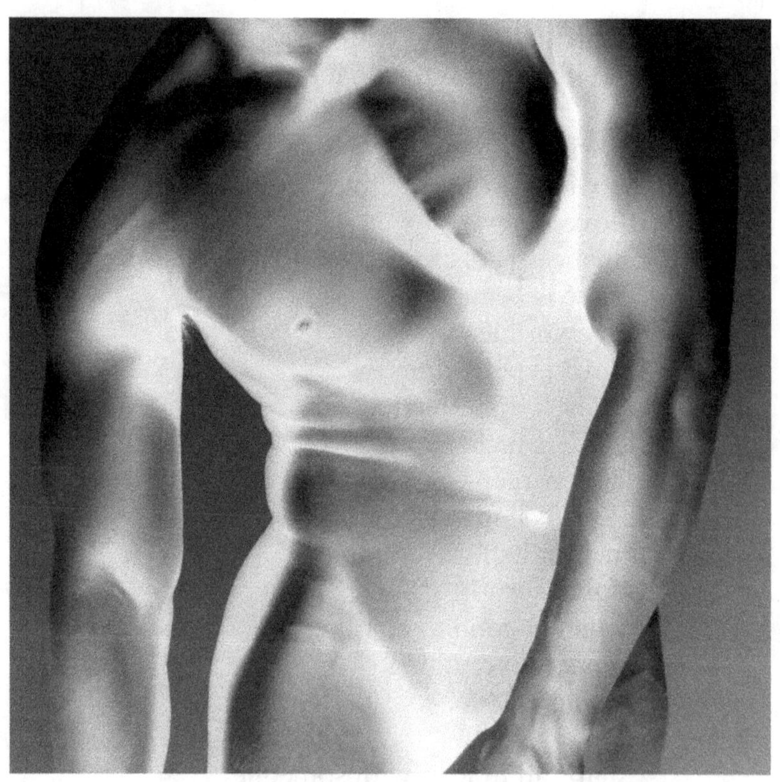

I endure myself

I endure myself

I endure myself.
I endure my selfsame fool.
I endure my selfsame foolish uncool doom.
I endure me being endurable to myself,
and it feels neither bad nor good.

I live dangerously.
I live in a folly full of dangers.
I live in a euphoric rally called dancing rangers.
I live dangerously enough to die cowardly,
but before that I wish to become a stranger.

I yearn for the impossible.
I yearn for the imperfectly reducible here and now.
I yearn for the perfectly irreducible power of no matter how.
I yearn for the impossibly done when the undoable
proclaim nothing in disclaiming everything aloud.

26

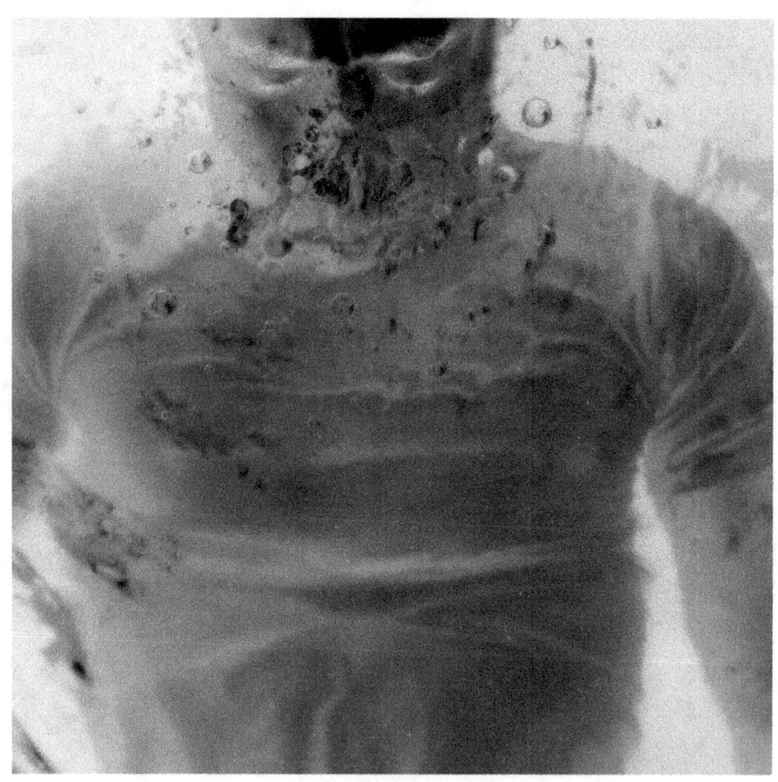

Happiness is an impossible dream

Happiness is an impossible dream
for intelligence:
                    how intelligent
ly,
     in the name of prison and freedom,
I miss sadness when I am on the verge!

I do sleep in a possible nightmare
called stupidity,
                    as long as the world
is satisfied in itself.
                         Nothing more
stupid will wake me up no matter what!

animals should still have to dream

animals should still have to dream

animals should still have to dream
when humans
have something worse
(than themselves) to lose
than evolving out of animals
no more.

animals should always do what they do
when humans are what they are.

the question is,
in the dream of
a fish,
what makes water water, but not fire?

the answer is,
i
who dream about another world,
do not bother to know the answer.

Beware, old fool!

Beware, old fool!

Beware, old fool!

If
you do not forget to be sad
as
a child does not remember to be happy,

but
you do laugh at your savoir vivre
as
a child does cry for its innocence,

I (any adjective)ly applaud
:
you have not lived in vain as a fool!

Wise

Everyone between birth and death
has one (self surviving) method,
otherwise
          (except those unwise),
the world learns to be less absurd.

Everyone beyond birth and death
has(will/did) the world to survive,
anywise
          (for those wise enough
to learn an absurd method), fine.

BUT

35

BUT

BUT
seems
(dis)satisfied between plus and minus,
(un)like a fish (un)aware of water.

BUT,

BUT
means
(dis)satisfaction beyond plus or minus,
(un)like water (un)aware of a fish.

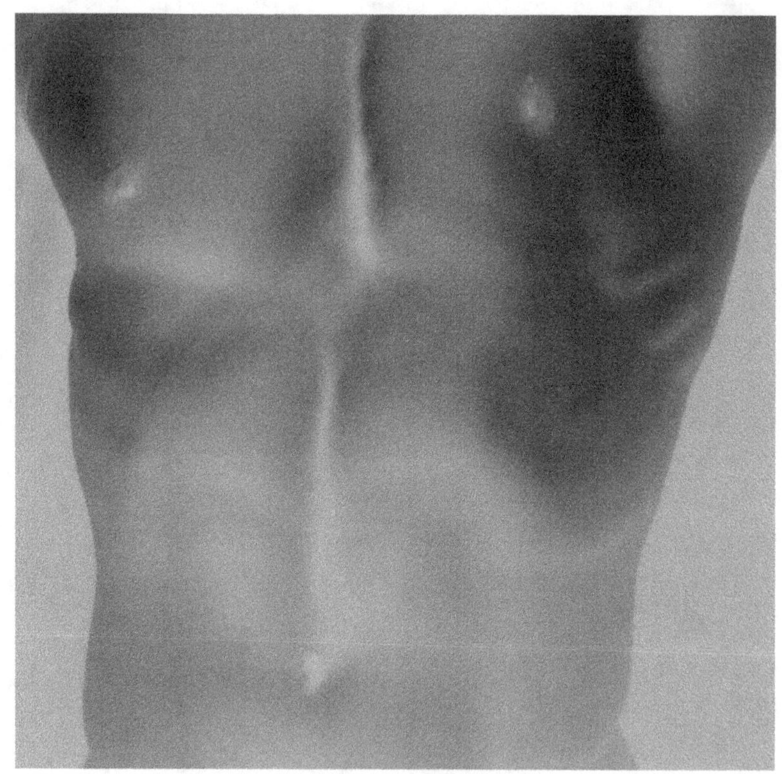

This or That, but never What

It is this or it is that,
but it so never is what I would it be.
I know why I still yet hope.
I ignore so I live on more.
I forget then I sleep till regret.
Times are everywhen it gets closely extreme
(close so much over me to undo the silver lining)
before it fails.
And I skin under all too human again.
I wonder yes the silver lining is the thing after if.

I am this or I am that,
but I surely never am what you love me for me.
I am sorry beyond your silence.
I am tired above your desire .
I am a failure sadder than your own.
I lose to find in the trying of the process to be not me
(or something cannot touch with values attached to)
before I give up.
Because I am why not an unordinary human.
I wonder yes I am only defined by your values after gold.

You are this or you are that,
but you by no means ever are what they fool by yourself.
You are reduced to a name.
You fake in the wrong face.
You are less free a day too late.
You rebel against the fair games out of the unfair rules
(even though fate is larger, deciding your death for your birth)
before one of them becomes you.
Alas, you are no different human.
You wonder yes you deserve not a better fate after the end.

Reasonably

Reasonably,
I do have
the same number of reasons
to die as to live.

Reasonably,
I did have
fewer reasons
to die than to live
until
I shall have
more reasons
to die than to live.

Reasonably,
I'd rather not have
any reason
to die or to live.

I almost hate to already love you

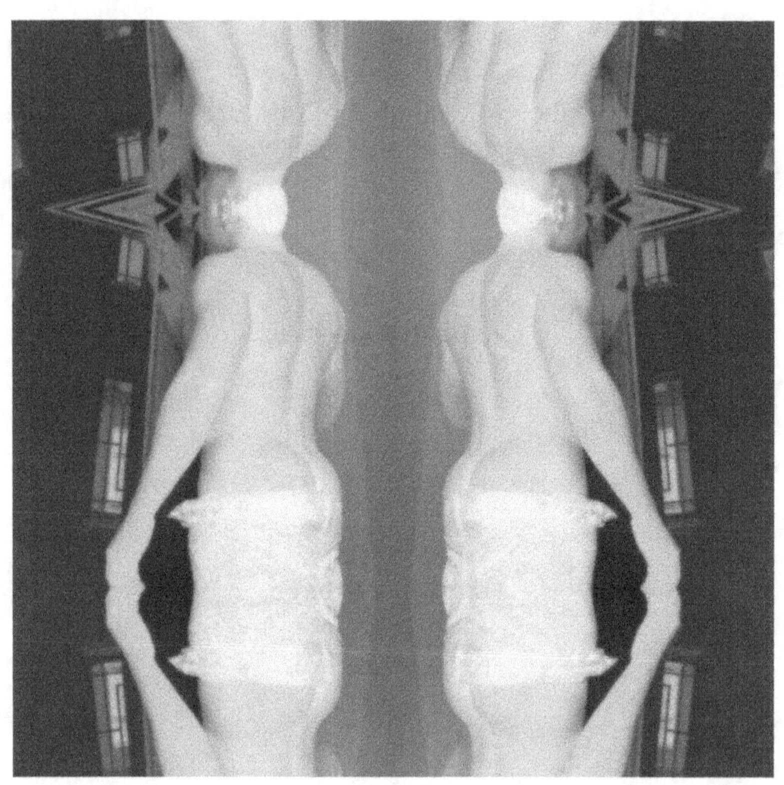

I almost hate to already love you

I almost hate to already love you,
either way as enforced as imagined,
either end no ifs, ands, or buts contingent,
I become the fear of being untrue.

I am an artist living more than worst,
against every happening beautified,
against not a single deceitful mind,
I release the concealed poetic verse.

I return into the nearest distance,
whereas mayhaps never promise morrows,
whereas perhaps time is made of sorrows,
I dissolve into the thickest absence.

When I am born in love

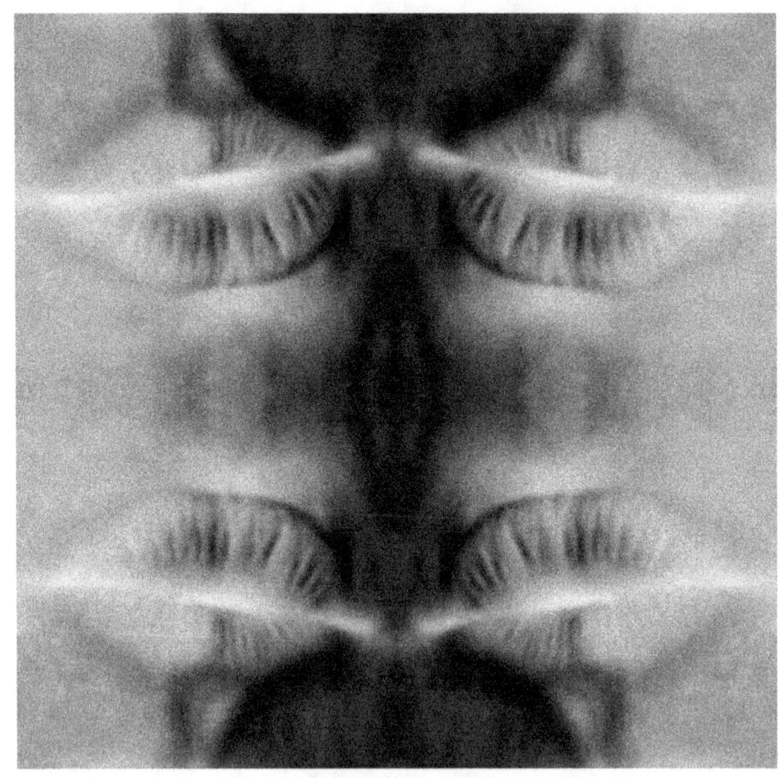

When I am born in love

When I am born in love with somebody,
with feelings found all over my body,
I have to sex the world to trust myself.

If (s)he is born in love much more indeed,
let feelings grow like spring in autumn leaves.

Life permitting, love inspirits sex.

When I am dead in love with somebody,
with feelings lost all over my body,
I have to sex myself to doubt the world.

If (s)he is dead in love absolutely,
let feelings morn the ends of all seasons.

Death forbidding, sex disheartens love.

44

Let's make love until

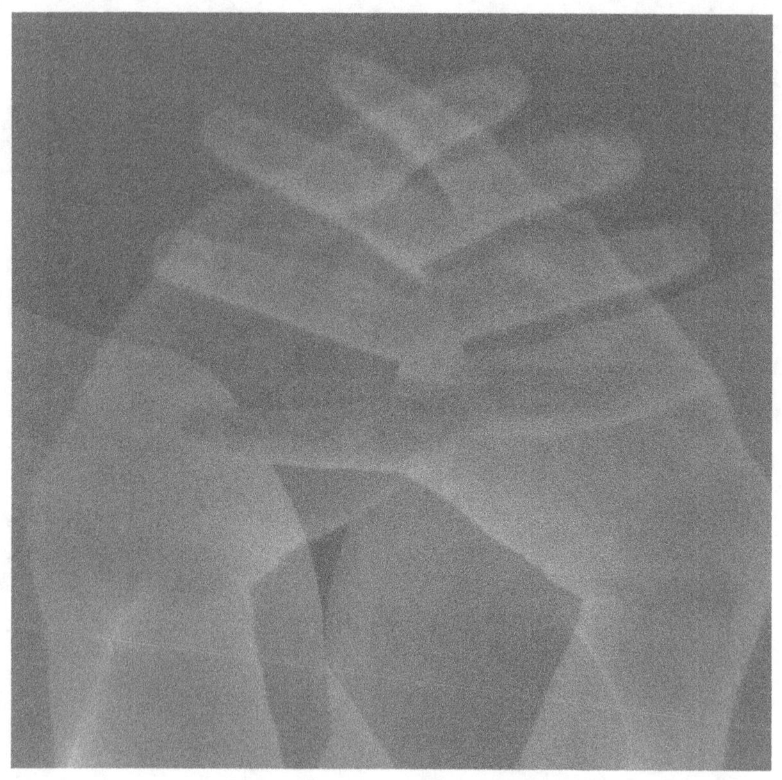

Let's make love until

Let's make love until

Let's make love until further until.

Until the end of the world, baby,
time has enough of us making love.

We are now each and every being
which feels more true than a fantasy.

The eyes of our eyes smile in their smiles,
becauseless sky falls on every why;
the ears in our ears fear of no scare,
since love appears as here as somewhere.

Let's make love until love makes itself.

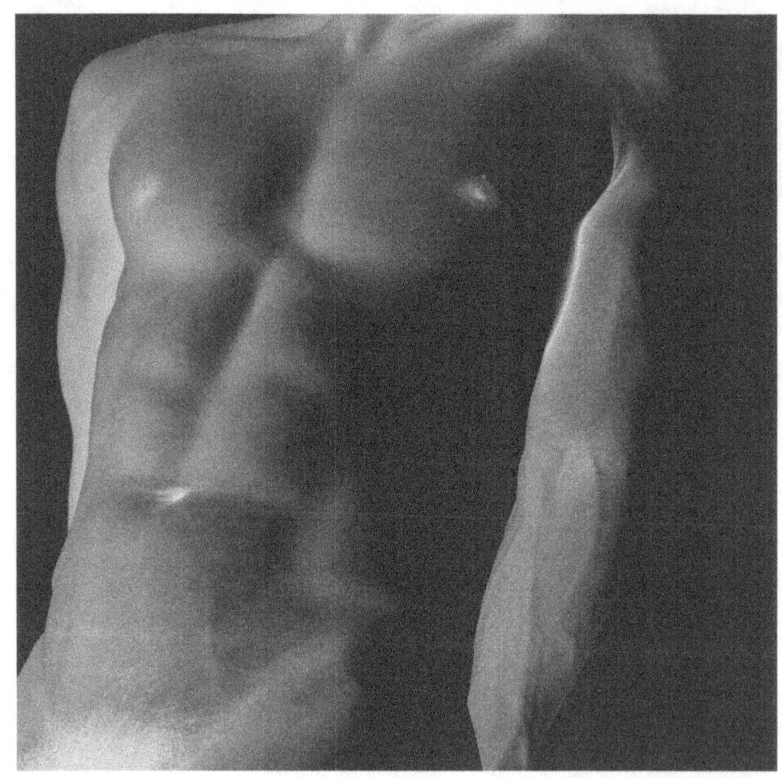

in the mood for poetry

in the mood for poetry on a frosty february morn.
wintry nostalgia lingers on in cuddling body warmth.
nature's insurgency resounds with the still glowing embers.
i float into a new reverie guided by your savour.

the serpent invades my yes & no with his muscular tongue,
my judgements have lost to my sensations many times around.
who said that pleasure is evil? i hunger for an apple.
electrified & stoned, i dance among erotic people.

driven by jealousy, you pull me out from the dancing pool
whose red-blooded rythmn is your heartbeat pounding on my foot.
reverie & your body are both my garden of eden
where reside numerous fantoms bearing heavenly powers.

the musical one peeking into our door is debussy
who was a drum played by picasso with imbecility.
soon it vapours into snow & falls down like piano notes,
our love is sewn by these notes & forms music of oath.

being alone in love

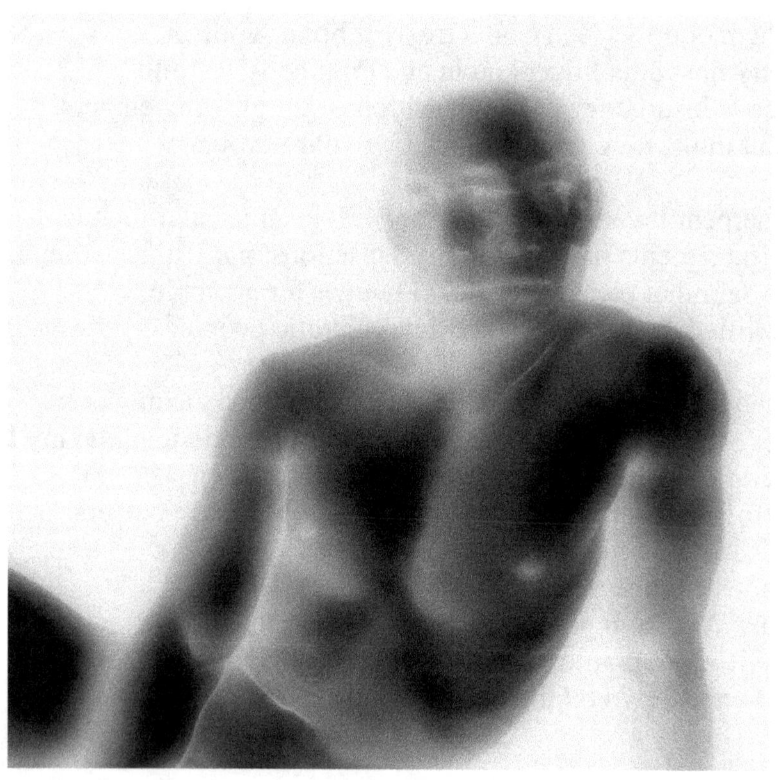

being alone in love

being alone in love
is as lonely as
being alone in pain.

hence,

when you are happy
somewhere in the world
at either day or night,

please understand
my loneliness
here and now.

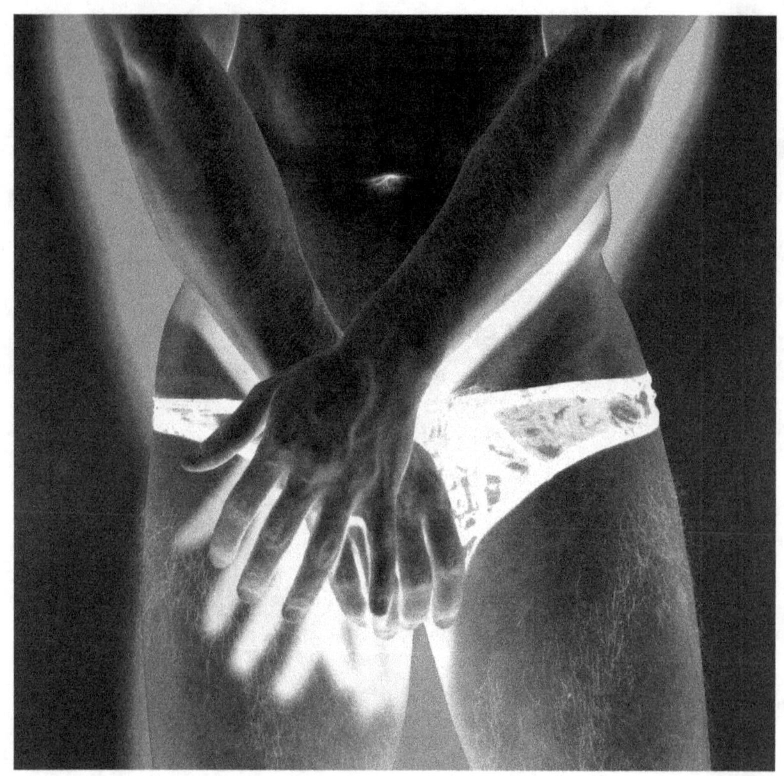

Only love may destroy me absolutely
and I should let it do the killing gently
(and it ought to die with me naturally),
if time had to become something else slowly.

Everything becomes time immediately
(at the same time everything changes really),
because death is the ultimate gravity
into which even death itself falls freely.

Still, nothing could live as love does perfectly
(perfection is much more deadly than lovely).

i fall in love with a devil

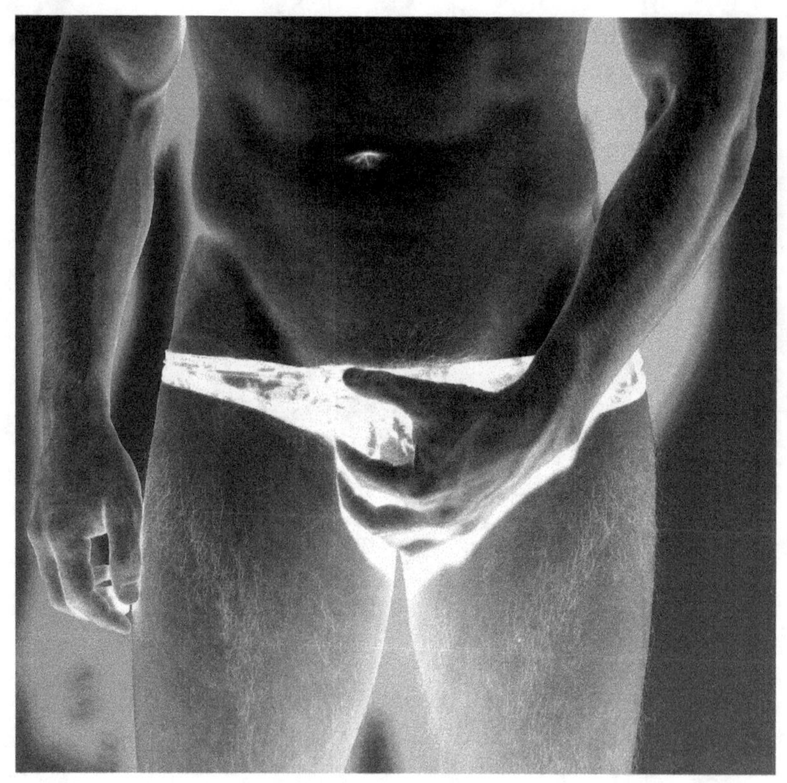

i fall in love with a devil

i fall in love with a devil,
then i become one myself
i do not envy an angel
when both of us live in hell

together, we are happy in pain
alone, miserable in freedom
desire is the food we feed on
jealousy, the air we breathe in

my wishes wish for your denials
your first yes resolves my last no
absolute kills every if between us
what we can yields to what we must

all true colors yearn to turn black
none of the stars miss their light
some nights overshadow a whole life
few days scorn how wrong seems right

knowledge makes little sense
this i should never know
feelings lie more or less
i learn to feel once more

i fall in love with you
then i become you
i die in love with you
so let me kill you

55

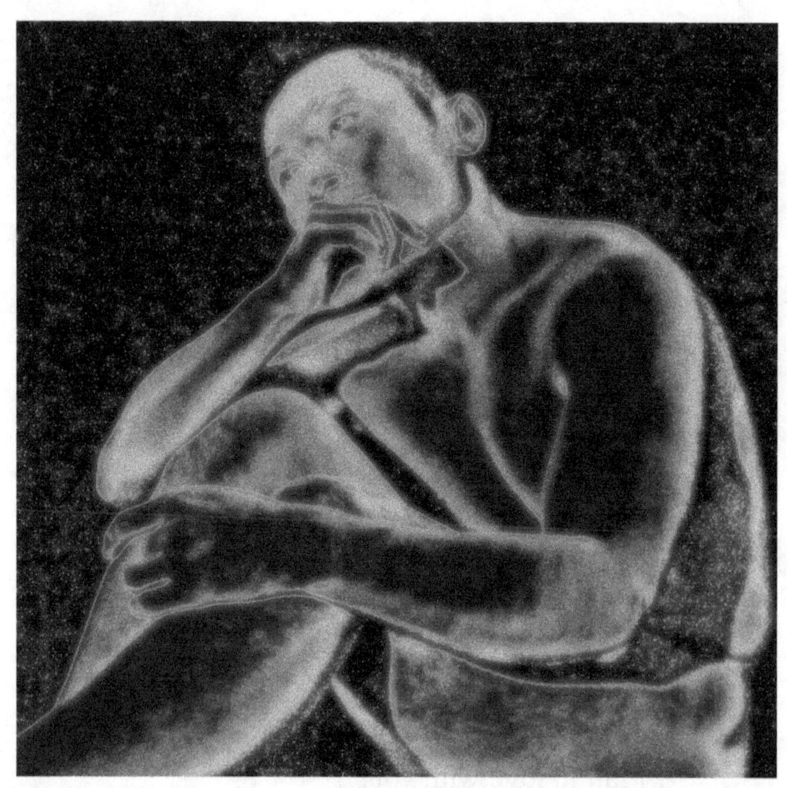

Funny how I feel sad now

Funny how I feel sad now and funny
how can I remember another word
(all words mean the same to all things) for love
(I do always remember to love you)?

Funny how I am in denial of
the weather freezing between you and me
like our love ageing from morning till night
(from night till morning either is lonely).

Funny how I remain happy no more
with my body disappoving my mind
(my soul approves nothing unknowingly)
who knows nothing but to retain your love.

And funny how love makes (only to break)
whatever it wishes to come untrue.

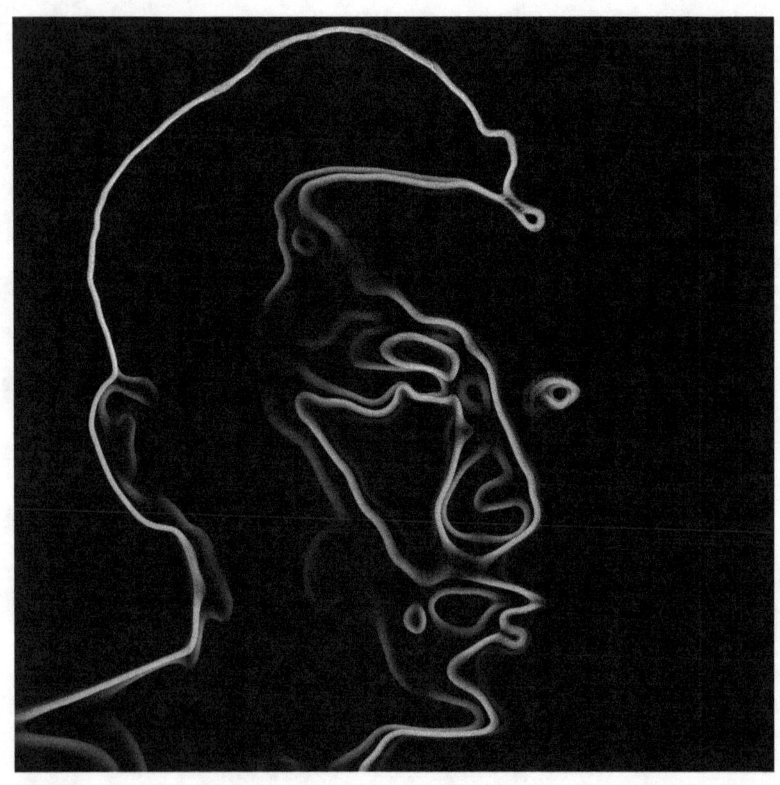

My Every Exhale

It would never last long enough to fail,
but the moment is strong enough to kill.
In my body freezes a loveless chill.
I could weigh my tears on the ocean's scale.

Our chapter is with your departure sealed,
now your new adventure has set sail.
I am powerless, trapped like a beached whale,
drying in the sun against my own will.

It did not last short enough to avail,
but the moment reaches forever, till
I know surely when you become unreal.
I breathe you out with my every exhale.

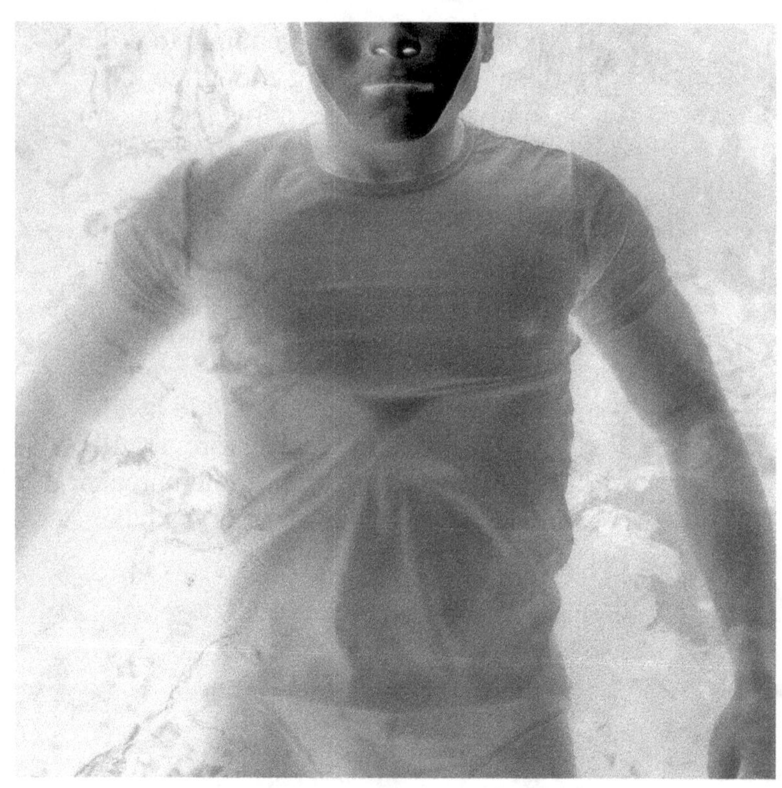

Value Of Gold

You are gold.

You may deny it,
others disregard it,
but I know it,
hence, you are mine.

You are gold covered by dirt,
still, I can hear your royal heart.
You are gold mistaken as rock,
because you never have the chance to shine.

You dream to be a diamond,
you worship the oriental jade,
you even envy silver, discreetly.
You have been wasting your fate.

You do not feel rooted where you are,
you do not feel alike with those who you are,
you do not feel yourself,
until a pair of golden hands find you
and lift you high under the sun.

Now you know, too,
that you are gold.

You realise it,
others appreciate it,
and I know it,
you are no longer mine.

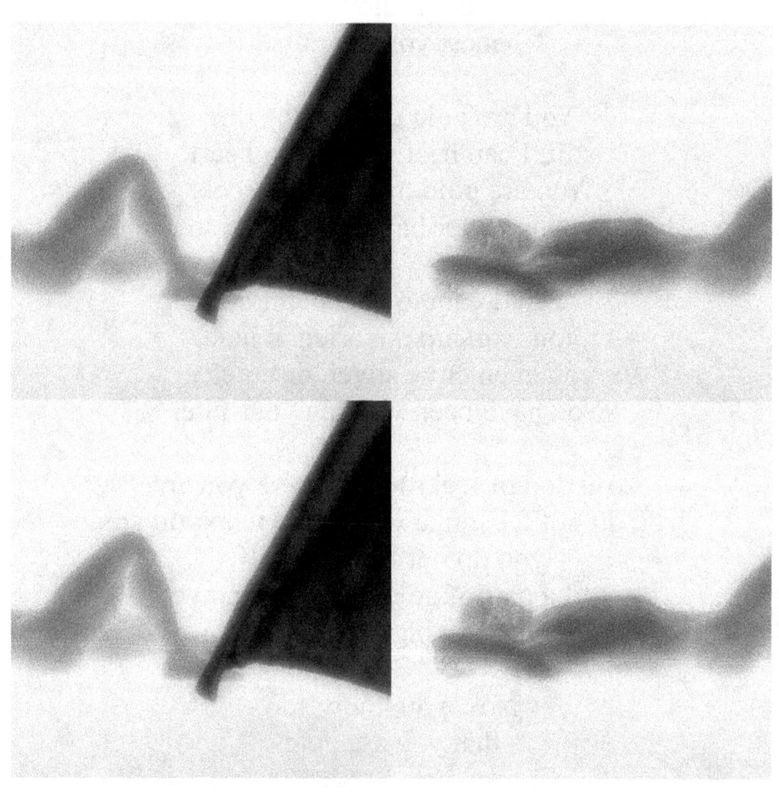

Solivagant

To die as I live: a solivagant.
No friend loves indeed, I am arrogant.
To be, or not to be: a mere pretence.
Truth could never trust in its own absence.

Do I suffer or do I appear glad?
What I deserve comes not from what I had;
what I desert goes back to where all end.
To a misfortune I but condescend.

Likewise, I breathe and move among the crowd
or would sooner lie down under the clouds
measuring the rhythm of my time left.
Let the big world grind, a sleep serves me best.

Best Friend

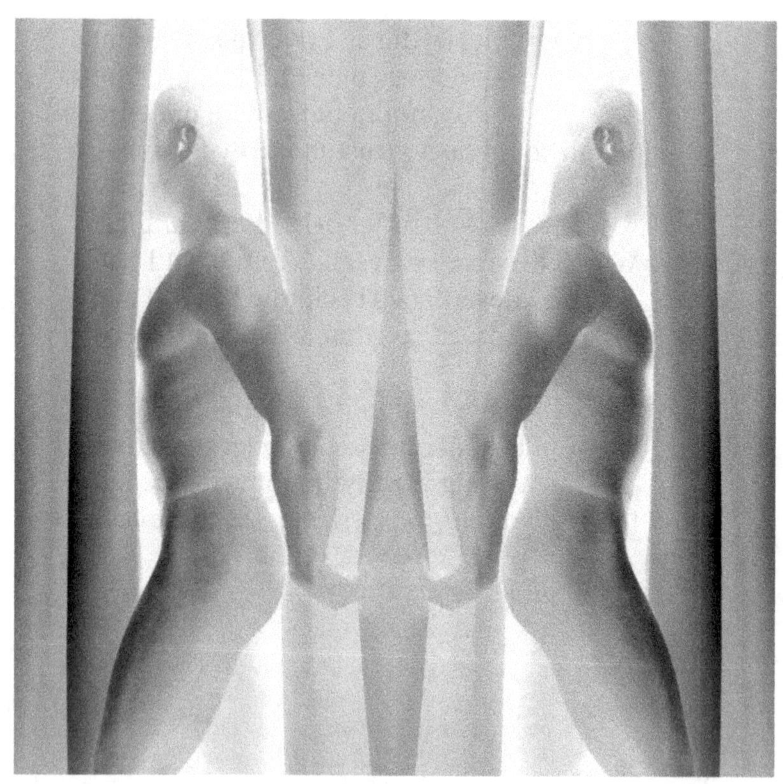

Best Friend

You introduced yourself as my friend,
the best friend I ever dream to have.
You thought everything on you depent,
everything I fail to understand.

Being hopeless and weak by myself,
I was joyful and true before you.
My feelings were what you made me feel,
you taught me the way I doubted, too.

Life treated me well, how curious!
Life was beautiful to me, I swear!
How a mind works is mysterious!
How the weather could change in the air!

With my imperfections getting old,
your impatience was growing faster.
Words and actions made a warm heart cold.
The yellow rose was ditched in the dirt.

A great wall builds itself between us,
whatever happends, it will not fall.
For good, the false friendship comes undone.
In a world of noises, no one calls.

shall i?

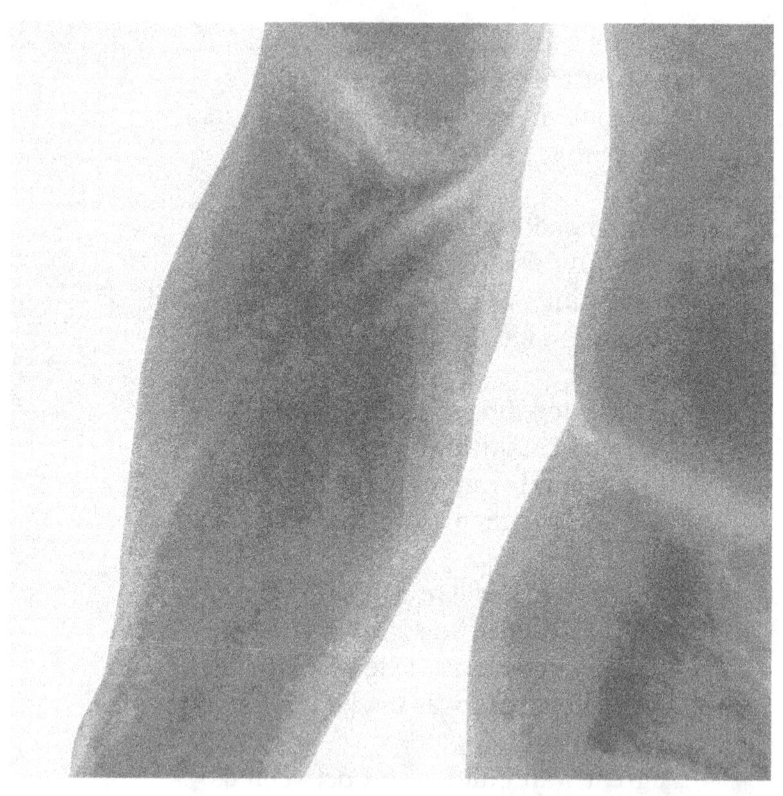

shall i?

shall i?
sleep in dreams to envy of thee
who dream in dreams of someone else
shall i?
sing the song of thy happiness
if thy sadness forgets my voice

shall i?
dare to crave something named freedom
when thou lead me into thy war
shall i?
glorify thy every season
though my spring promises much more

shall i?
ask and tell thee why i have hopes
with or without which thou art fine
shall i?
live thy life losing my purpose
for my fate is sealed despite thine

Despite me being anything

Despite me being anything

Despite me being anything but music,

it had been
                snowing snow
as it had never been,
it was
        raining snow
unseasonably,
it is
        raining rain
as it should, could, would be,
it will be
                snowing rain
miraculously,

in the time of my life that excludes me.

Further back; Closer enough

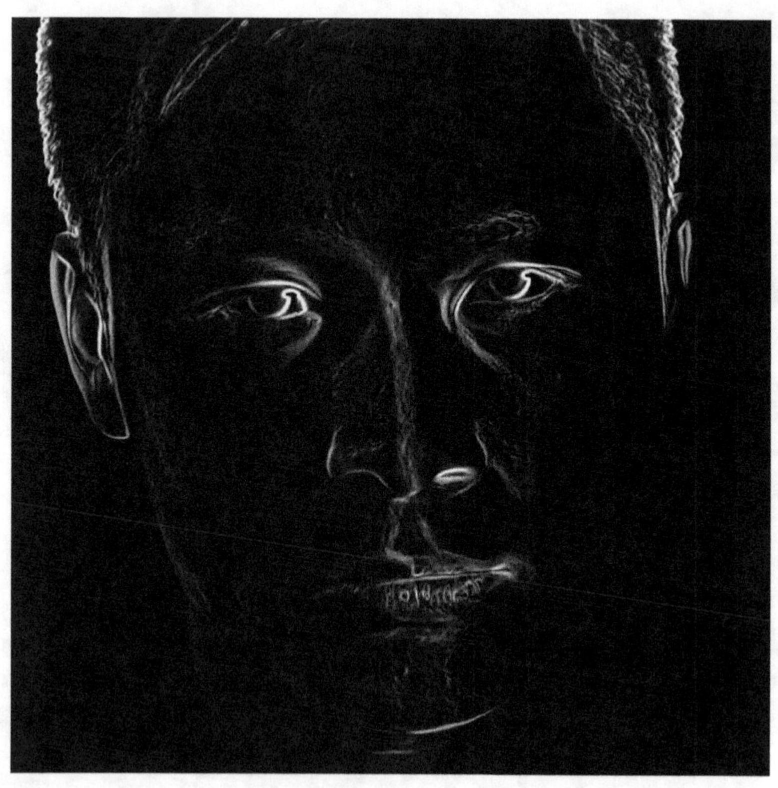

Further back; Closer enough

Further back; Closer enough

Further back,
        as far as is time,
                    a boy
believed a misbelief
                until
no doubt had doubted life,
                    yet still
the best tragedy ridiculed each choice.

Closer enough
            to feel unloved,
                        two souls
convict their alliance,
                    therefore
distance smells of dry blood
                        before
egos lose touch with selflessness they owe.

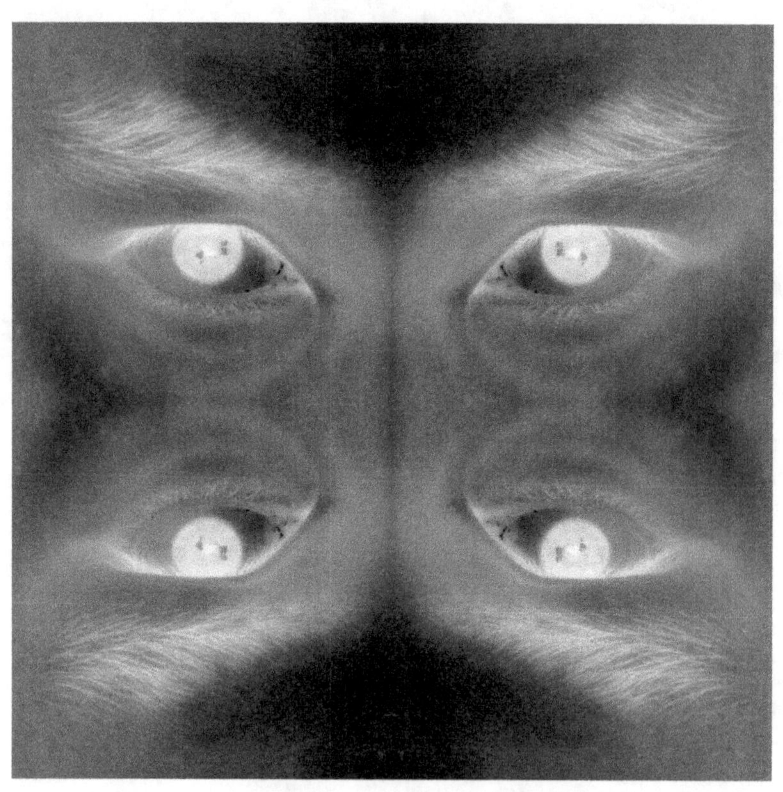

Fear

Fear

Fear, I know you well, at this moment
when the entire world is losing me.
You are more real than a mother's tears
and less simple than my poetry.

Tomorrow wants to be forgotten
among the stars in this deep midnight;
yesterday was a beautiful curse,
even though everything seemed pure white.

I am at war against space and time,
I surrender to reality.
Love is hidden, but not to be found.
I ask: why it has to be like this.

The unknown turn absolute somehow.
I, being wide awake, dream to sleep.
Timely, fear, you should be over now.
After all, I feel free, falling deep.

after all my sleep has been slept

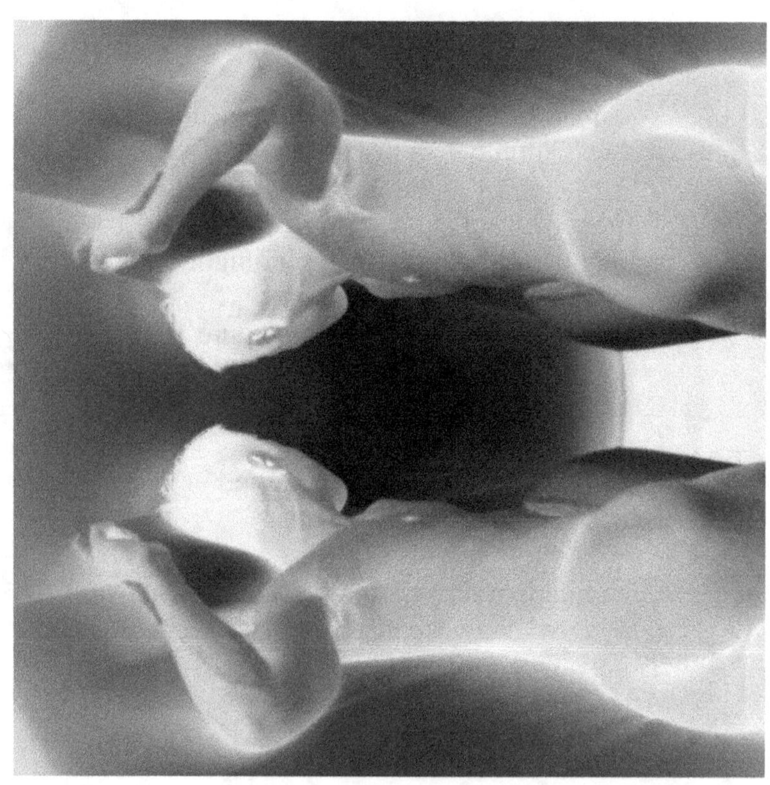

73

after all my sleep has been slept

after all my sleep has been slept
i still wonder why i needed to sleep
i still wonder why i needed to think
after all my thoughts have been thought

after all my flames have been burnt
i still ponder why i have been frozen
i still ponder why i have existed
after all my life has been lost

i was not invited

i was not invited

i was not invited

i was not invited until
red wished blue,
yellow faked purple

and bythetimewhen
white lost its pure,
i did care enough no more

When my anger gets old and weak

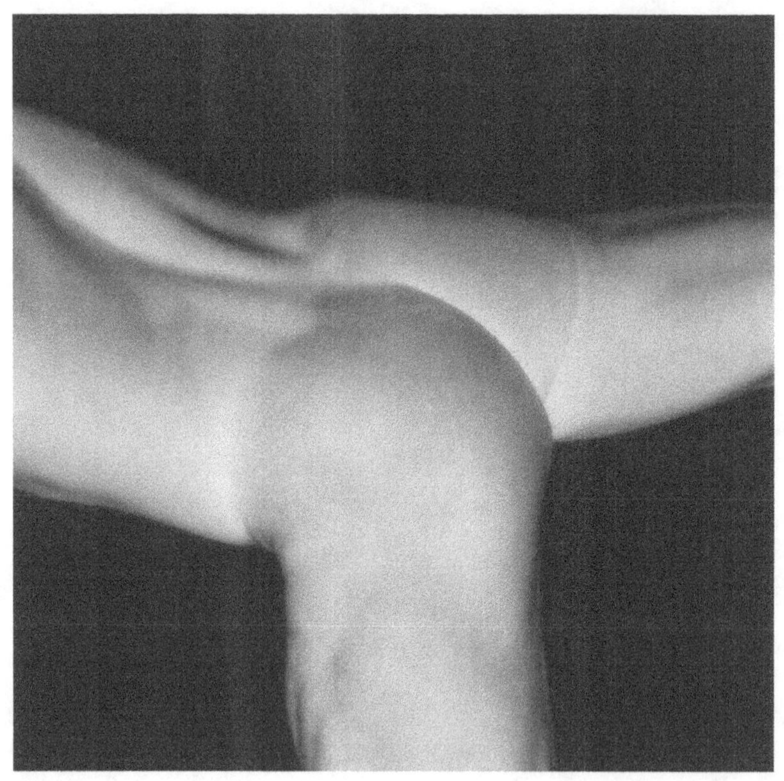

When my anger gets old and weak

When my anger gets old and weak,
I am already old and weak
like dry grass on my very tomb.

Here comes a new life in the womb,
destined for both good and bad. Sigh,
when its dreams awake themselves, sigh,
when its anger ceases to be...

The truth that untruths cannot be
tells enough lies to everyone:
another sun is yet undone.

hope(help)less

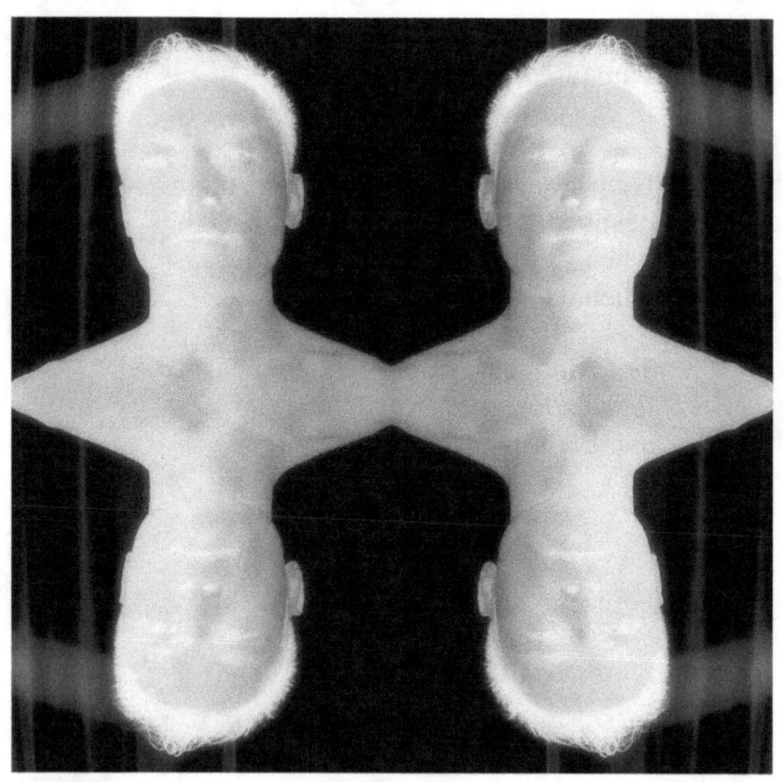

hope(help)less

hope(help)less

hope(help)less is a two-headed ness.

with one head sucking its own toe,
the other fucking its own hole,
it grows into a hope(help)ful fool.

an unhope(unhelp)ful who gets horny
whenever hope(help)lessness gets brainy
regardless of its two heads without brains.

all the same, a hope(help) hope(help)s in vain.

i am why before

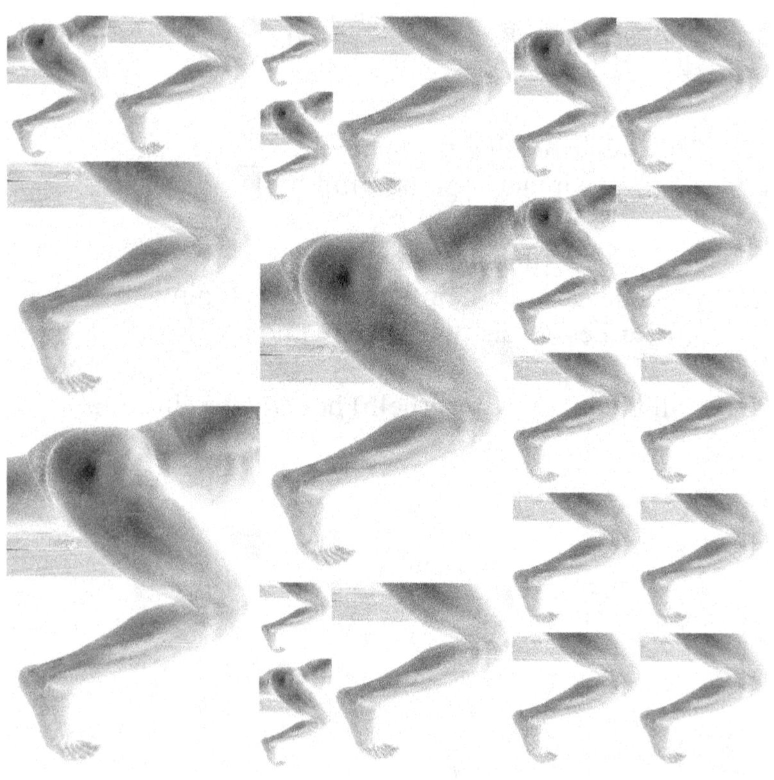

i am why before

i am why before who is whenandwhere,
small is big enough, long is almost short,
howtobe knows little, new finds the old way,
nothing hides all, truth tells lies without doubt.

what the hell is that if which is not this?
fake is unsure of the questions unmasked,
deeming everything could be fine although
time wakes up the darkness despite the dusk.

so hereandnow is more faithful to none,
less measurable than sky wants to drop,
a farther dream meanwhile a nearer done,
as silence to voice as bottom to top.

most never rejects forevermore but
best will always welcome betterorworse.
together we let karma touch our fate,
through joy and grief we understand the curse.

in the face of

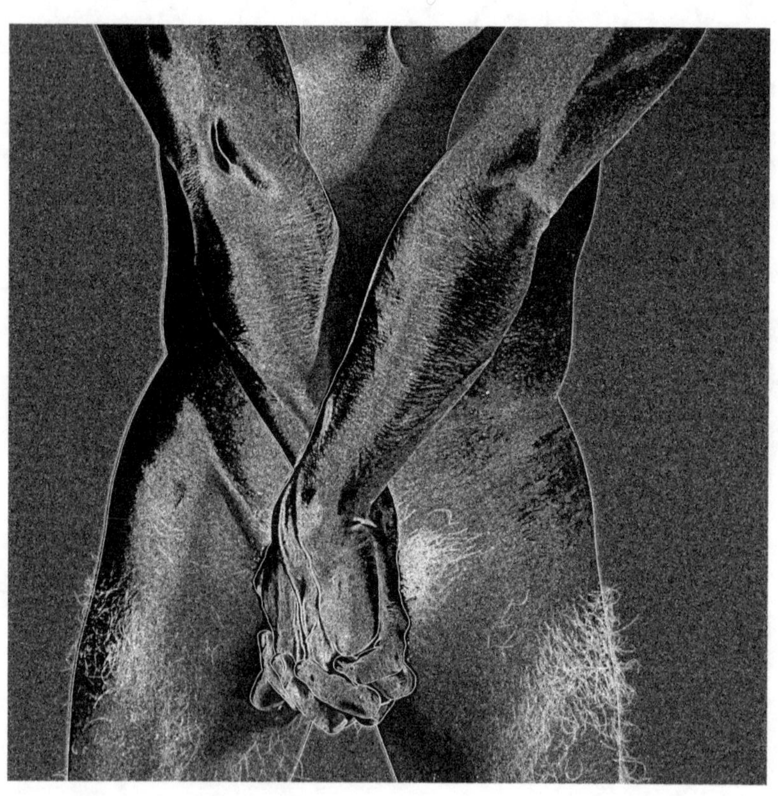

in the face of

in the face of ugliness beyond pain
beauty defends all virtues except when
human nature must answer nature's call
and humanity being most cruel

in the lap of poverty failing greed
wealth reaches faster than nearer a grave
human rights are buried in right and wrong
and animals dig up bones every spring

in the name of shame next to betrayal
glory lies to fool who seem less loyal
human diseases cure human cultures
and a good doctor saves a bad preacher

in the words of death killed by final no
life floats nowhere high before sinking low
humanunkind is still one of a kind
and a body survives without a mind

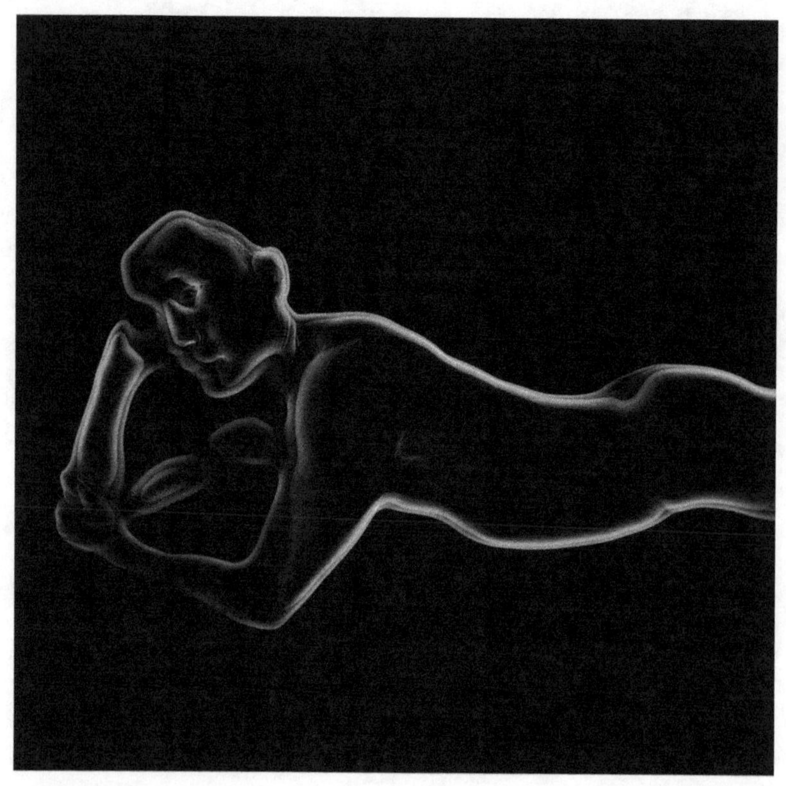

Whether by way of

Whether by way of living in dying,
birth and death are merely happen to be,
or behind a hoping yes, each no doubts;
Time derides dreams until the last heartbeat.

Whether by way of proving nothing false
before the doom, the ground turns to the sky,
or into some wisdom's pride cracks a fool;
Someone sees some no one under the skin.

Whether by way of saying less but more,
november recounts its petals in june,
or the sun confides itself to the moon;
All that breathe and walk do not imagine.

Whether by way of kissing a shadow,
lost memories must return as stories,
or low climbs high meanwhile above falls down;
Every morrow is due to be buried.

Should a dream forget a whole life

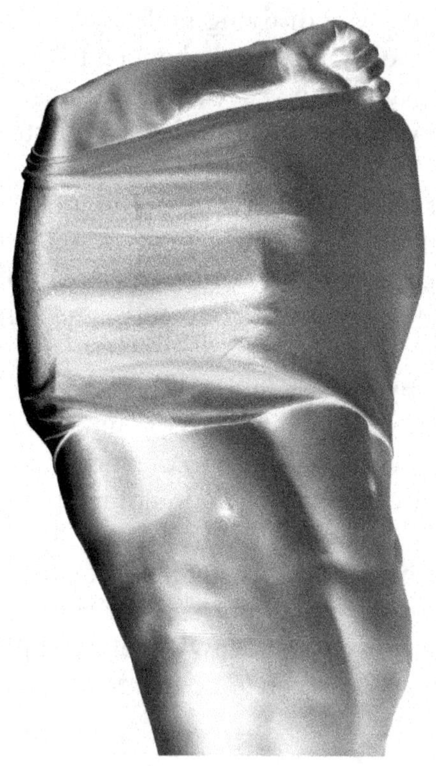

Should a dream forget a whole life

Should a dream forget a whole life,
        a handful contain more than five,
        a friendship smile to a sharp knife,
        a husband give birth for his wife,
your every failure could be mine.

Should freedom be compulsory,
        stupidity voluntary,
        both truth and untruth luxury,
        fame and fortune solitary,
sadly, the world would be happy.

Should time have to redeem from age,
        heaven reach no god through a bridge,
        love and hate play mutual judge,
        spirits vanish as a mirage,
the core must flow outside the edge.

NOTHING, NOBODY, NOWHERE, NEVER

NOTHING
is desired to be justified before death.
travellers from (after)life, slaves of TIME&SPACE,
what esle could feel more (un)real than the ageing youth?
MUST&SHALL would rather consumate WAR&PEACE.

NOBODY
is out of the whole world, within a single hair,
holding (as if) mindfully the prodigal son
who feels (the moment he understands HOPE&FEAR)
that all fade in vain, thus there comes another dawn.

NOWHERE
is opposite of (WHERE) being in existence,
regardless, against ODDS&EVENS, steals the thief
of destiny each impossible allowance.
have we suffered enough from (un)requited self?

NEVER
is (re)occurring between indeed and perhaps,
but FOREVER remains as trustful as a fool.
TOMORROW does no harm as long as TODAY sleeps
through YESTERDAY(among many days only few).

Had you not loved me

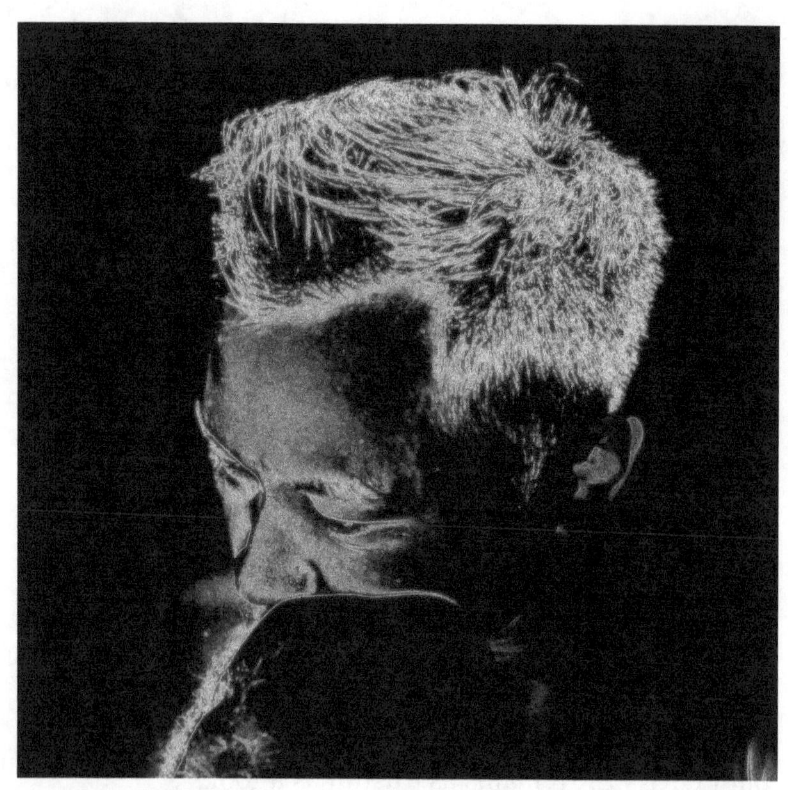

Had you not loved me

Had you not loved me
as much as you did
and
did I not miss you
as much as I do...

Had you abandoned me,
had your duty disowned me,
and
had I not saddened you,
had my life reassured you...

Had you been hated by some,
misunderstood by none
and for you
had I not been the only one,
the end of your very own luck...

Between your love and my freedom,
I must choose the latter

Now
both you and your love are lost,
I know
no more where I am headed
nor less where I am from.

i shall be missing you

i shall be missing you

i shall be missing you
even more than
i should have loved you
then
but did not

i shall be missing you
as much as
i cry, missing you
now
but did not

i shall be missing you
no less than
i shall be hating myself
for the rest of my life
but did not

If I have to cry

95

If I have to cry

If I have to cry, I'll cry like a man
whose father is the child in every man;

I'll cry like a child less fearing life,
more needing and craving love
from the entire world which knows
how to cry for every man;

I'll cry like myself in tears so true,
and in truth so tearful,
until I forget who I am,
then remember: I am every man.

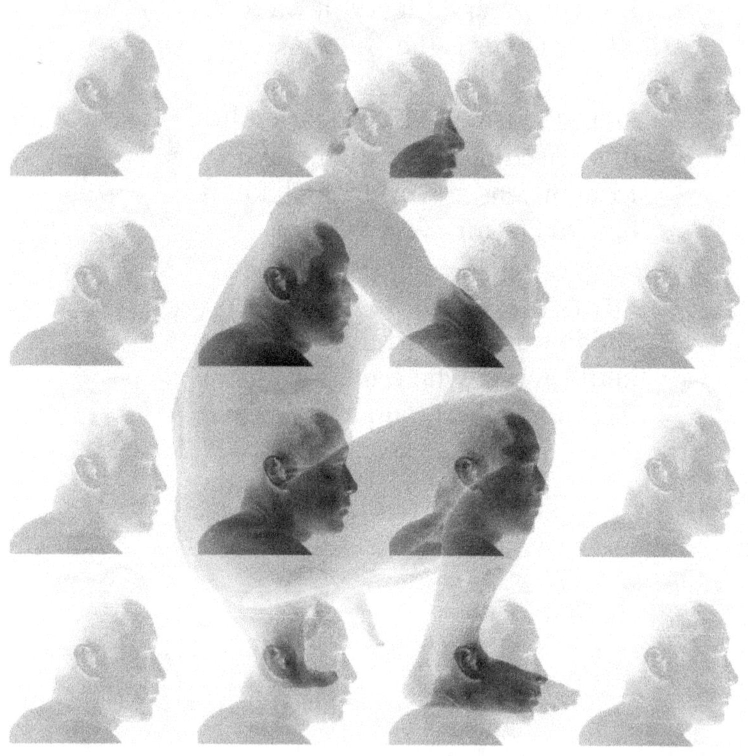

a heart; a home

a heart
wherein
silence fills emptiness,
dreams the dream of
a hope in hopelessness,
among stolen thieves
under fallen leaves,
a heart
resides inside someone
homeless.

a home
whereof
shadow flees consciousness,
walks the walk of
a time in timelessness,
against the pride of
a self-proclaimed prince,
a home
trembles outside someone
heartless.

My soul is real

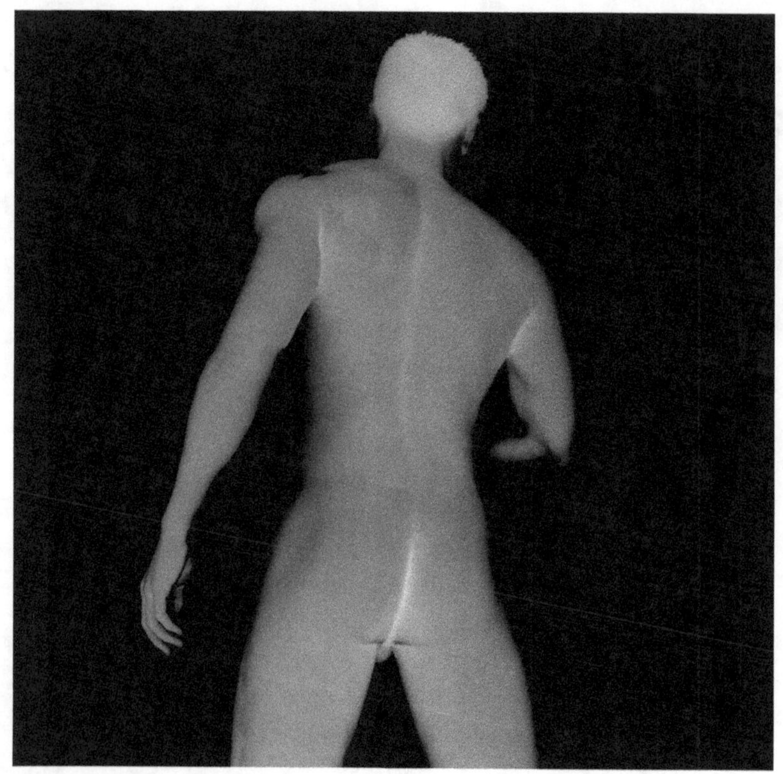

My soul is real

My soul is real if winds could move mountains.
I am moved by the wind which was a tree
growing into a forest. And the wind
has stopped blowing to grow into the sea.

My soul finds home wherever the wind rests.
Whatever the wind grows to be, is me.
Breathing and living for a thousand years,
I am the wind whenever I am free.

He

He

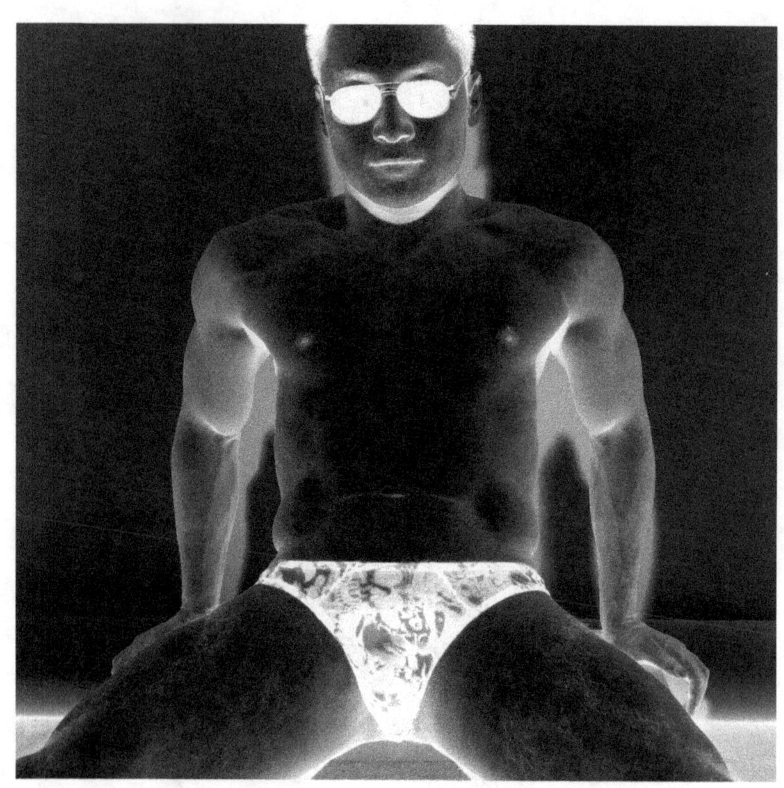

101

He

He lies in the silence of yesterday,
until spring rain grows summer in his hair.
Eyes mistake golden days for autumn rays.
Tears are forgotten when fresh smiles sound rare.

Glib promises echo between swift lips,
somewhere in time sleeps a truthful dreamer.
Today was tomorrow that did not leap,
what could have been still feels so near.

Doubts are frozen, leave winter to the moon;
faith is reborn in an instant of fire.
A butterfly pops out, goodbye, cocoon!
Over the mountain he can fly higher.

Be the color of the sky, be the Man,
for the night failed to darken your desire.
Break free from your imperfections, be bad,
be the Master of the land, be the Sire!

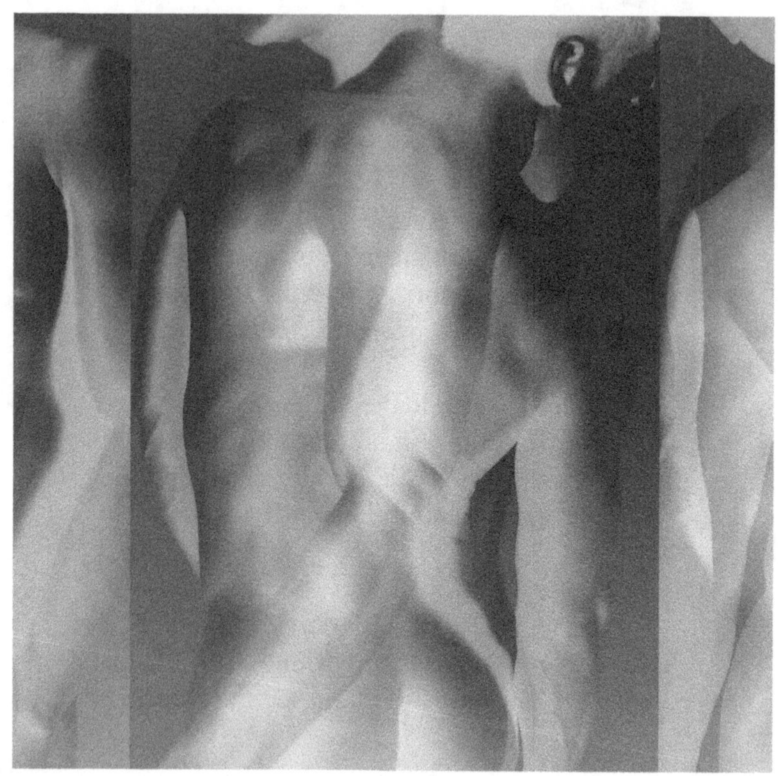

May has been born out of April

May has been born out of April
in a green circulating mode,
both being poems that time
and space never finish writing,
when he (Spring is un
seasonably jealous of
a poet asleep
who can be anything,
anywhere,
                anytime)
wakes to sleep, sleeps to wake
and sleeps again, until wakes.

Enjoy! Yes! Enjoy!

Enjoy! Yes! Enjoy!

Enjoy! Yes! Enjoy!

It is because
          love
(the beautifulest
              accident
                    of the universe)
might only flourish in joy,

should you need a reason to destroy
the fragilest
            rules
               of the universe
that forbid you to enjoy.

Apart from his being featureless

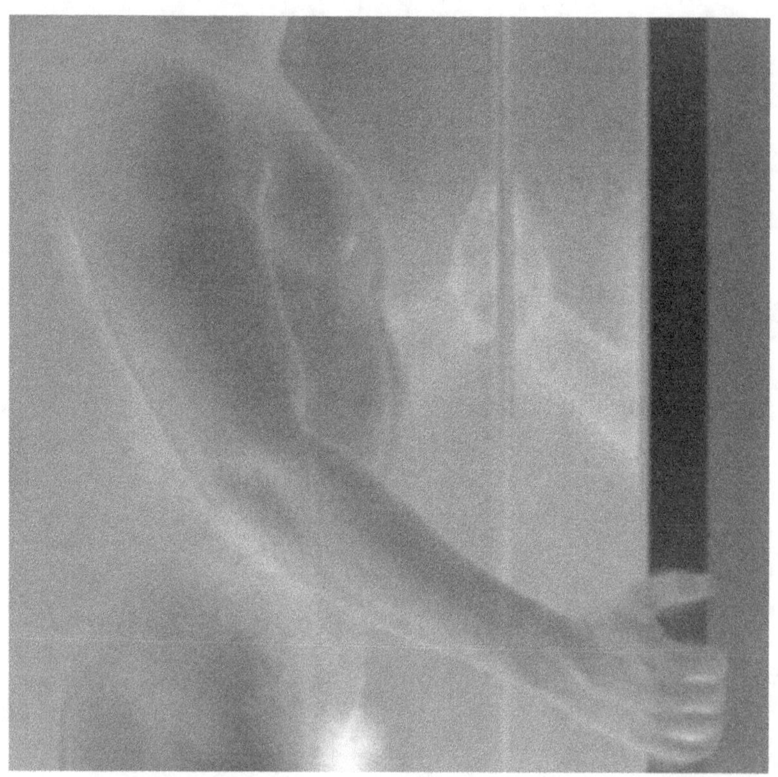

Apart from his being featureless

Apart from his being featureless,
all his doings naturalise less
conscious creatures than his undoings.

Unconsciously, he fears the ending
beginning of everything dying
(everything living moves everywhere,
nonetheless time stays to be unfair)
consciously in front of its own fear.

In front of his own fear dare features
entirely created in nature.

all is num6er

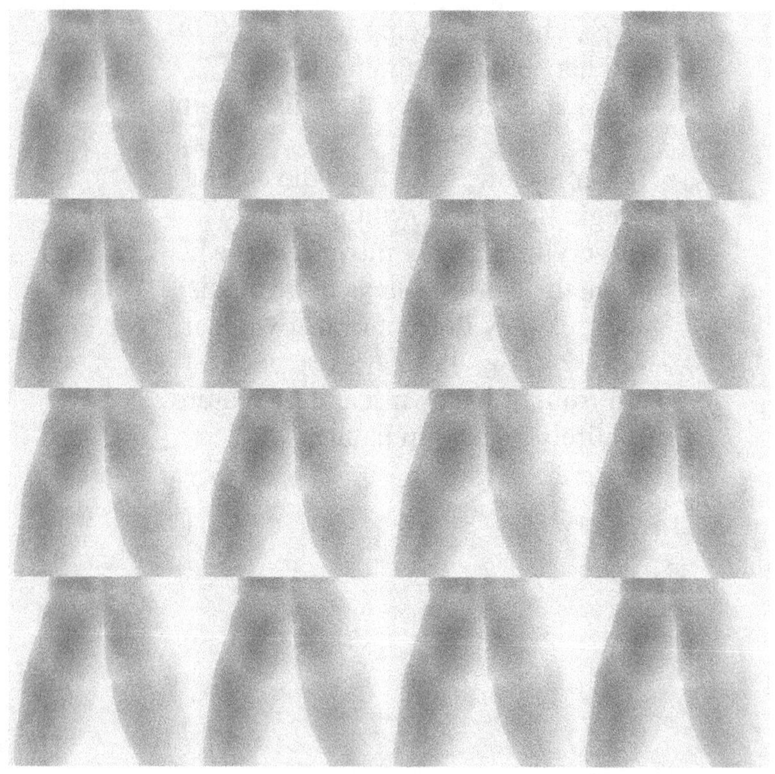

all is num6er

all is num6er

all is num6er.

10v3 disco4ers
                i7self
                    (lo5t in a nu4ber,
fou2d in ano4her)
                  without any hel9
which count5 to be
ma7hemat1c8lly help2ul.

10v3 is n8mber
0n3(, 2, 3, 4, 5, 6, 7, 8, 9 till
                              after
numbe5 n0n3).

10v3 is all
in a world where all is 10v3.

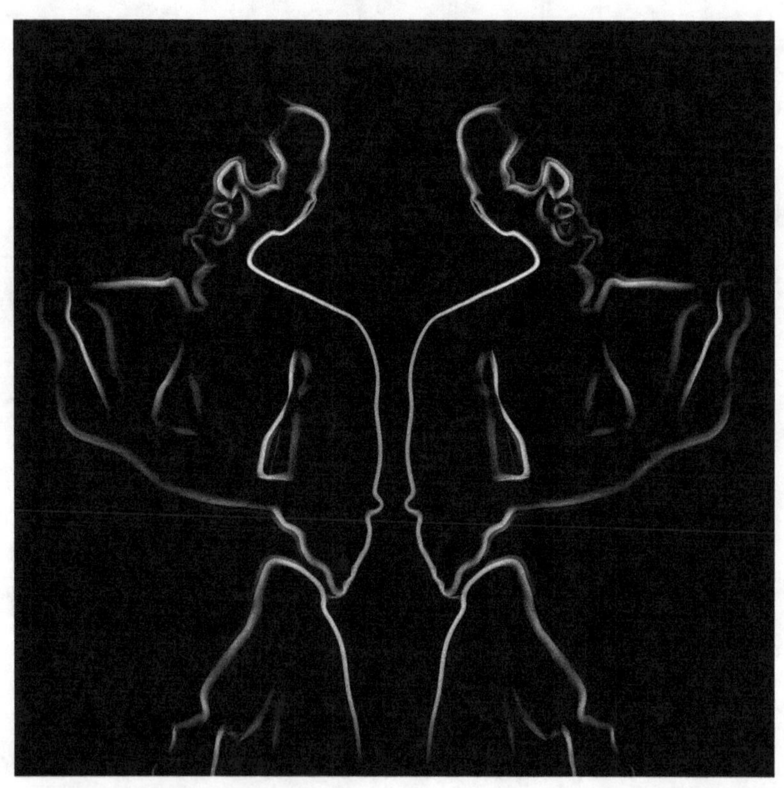

The world and I

The world and I,
neither being secretly lost in both,
are both openly found in neither.

The world and I,
neither being aimlessly sad in both,
are both willfully gay in neither.

The world and I,
neither being certainly no in both,
are both doubtingly yes in neither.

The world and I,
neither being humanly sick in both,
are both socially sane in neither.

Do I want what I think I want?

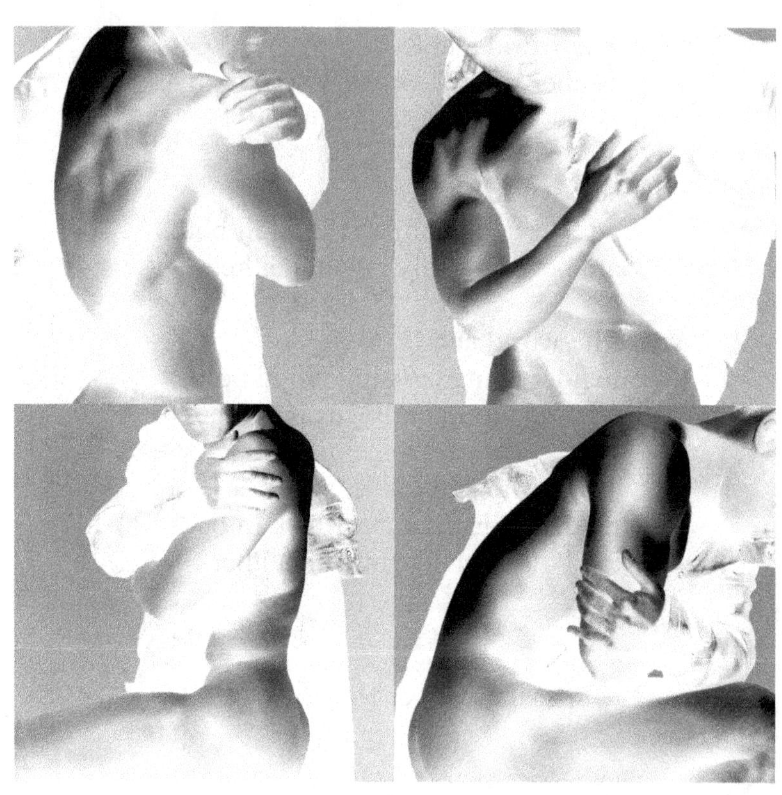

Do I want what I think I want?

Do I want what I think I want?

The worthless room feeling enormous,
the elephant shows somewhere else.

I want, therefore I think.
I think, therefore I want.

The elephant hides somewhere else,
the enormous room feeling worthless.

Do I think what I want to think?

ridiculous

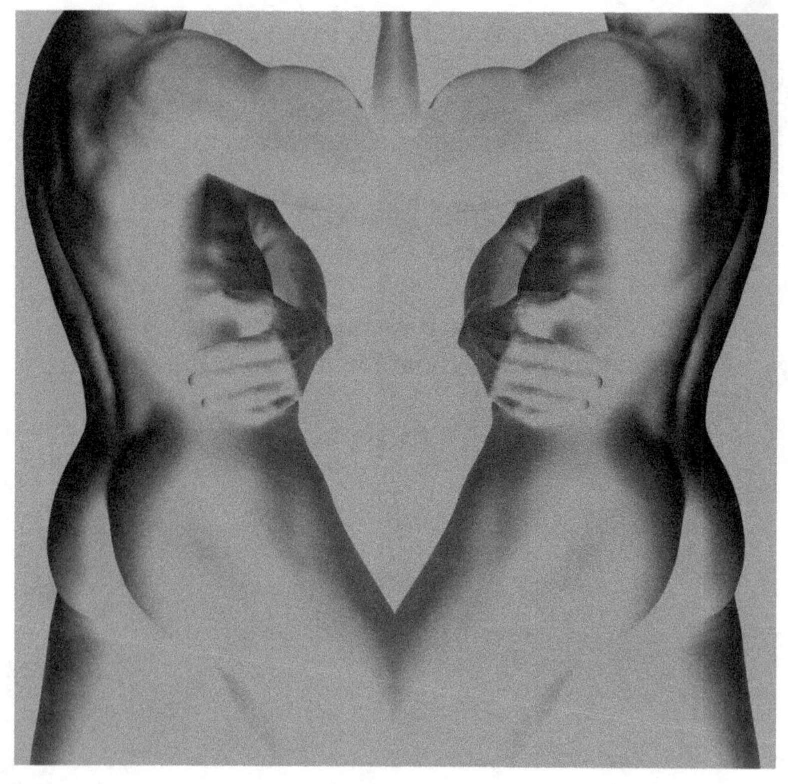

115

ridiculous

everything is ridiculous
YES,
i say everyone, everytime, everywhere

everyone is ridiculous
YES,
i say everytime, everywhere, everything

everytime is ridiculous
YES,
i say everywhere, everything, everyone

everywhere is ridiculous
YES,
i say everything, everyone, everytime

if debussy envies

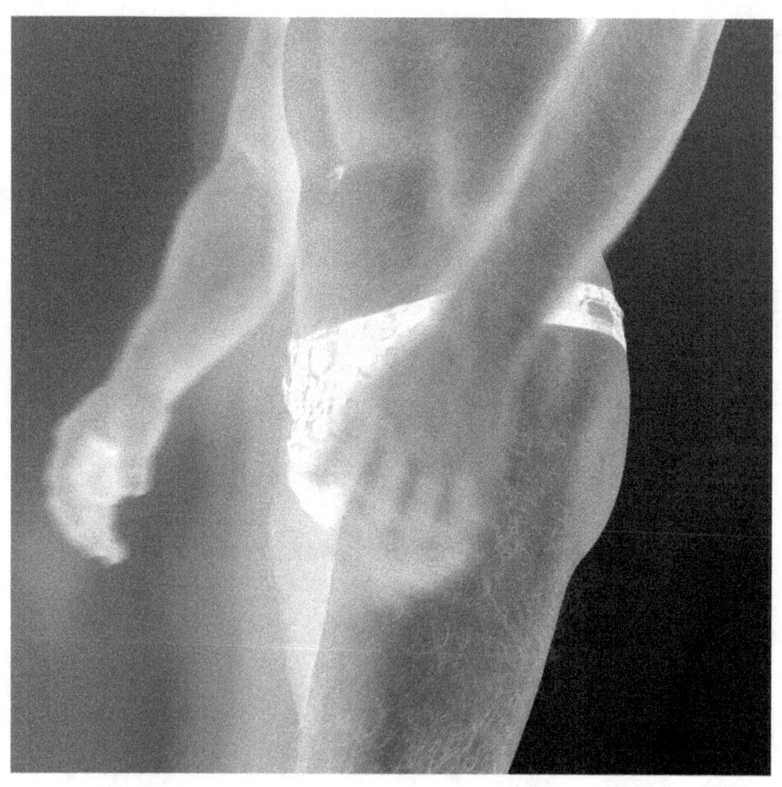

if debussy envies

if debussy envies a nobel mind
of any unmusical kind,
sounding deaf deserves more than looking blind.
true is dream;
now feels such death as life,
fire is ash;
near fills such ground as sky,
regardless of the world we deny,
already past leaves future behind.

if computers detest all human acts
of every unanimal fact,
clever skills procure less than stupid tacts.
red is blood;
art loves such peace as war,
dusk is light;
trash shows such crime as law,
nonetheless the universe grows, packed
with yet to be nonsensed artifacts.

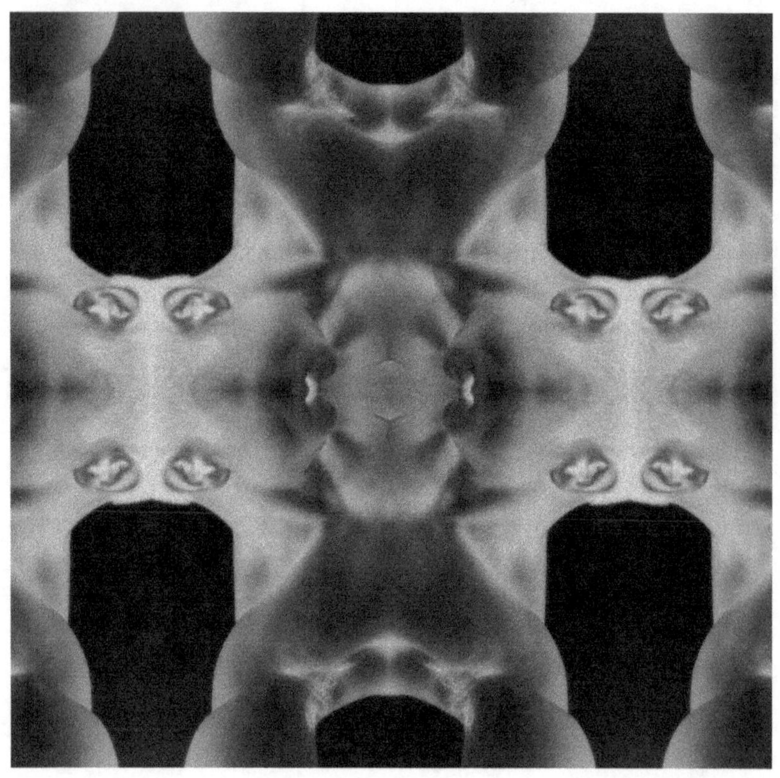

who-many-T

I have no face
in who-many-T,
never did,
never will.
Those beezy fantasizing Mars
surely do,
surely did,
surely will.

Whether earth is
1+1 good or 1+1 bad,
or Mars is
not red(black or white)
enough;
whether earth is
1+1 near or 1+1 far,
or Mars is
neither here nor there,
we fail;
whether earth is
1+1 soon or 1+1 late,
or Mars is
still, yet, however,
(un)known,

history, now and future
taste
        the same
                blood.

He is objectified as prey in flesh and bones,
causing electrical titillations
through the body of a lion,
who has been languishing
since the crow at dawn.
In its mind, a thirst
for feverish blood
of the savanna.

I am this lion.

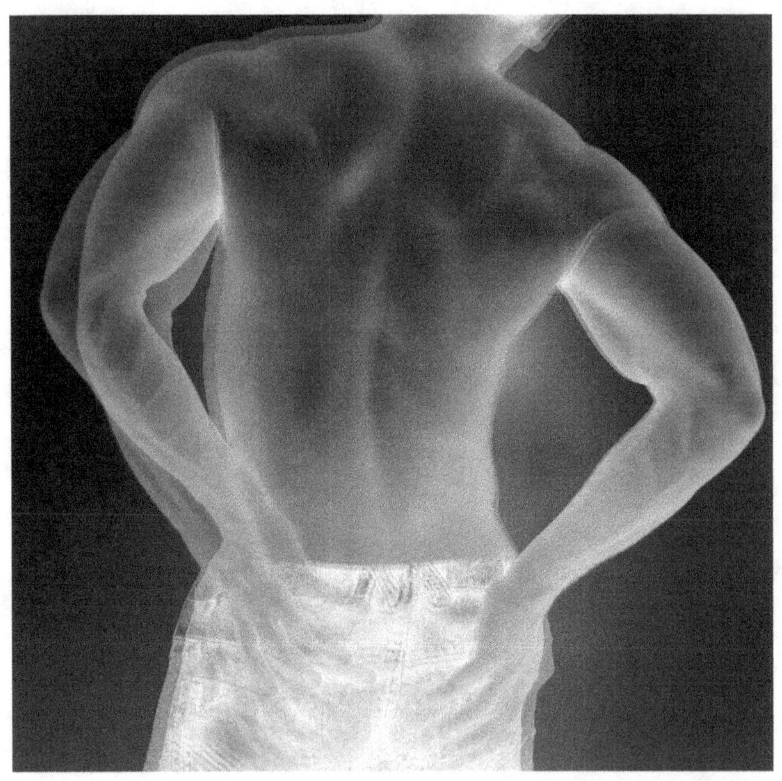

Come to me

Come to me, as primitive as you are:
Your uneducated language
manhandles any Shakespeare;
Your offensive blink electrifies me;
Your graceless gesture
spares the laughable hypocrites no excuse;
Your untrimmed body hair
symbolises your brimming hormones,
and it smells the real life to me.

Come as an animal claiming its prey:
I hunger to be your prey,
powerless yet enticed,
surrendering to your muscular limbs.
And withal the god between your legs
is the only devil I worship.
He makes my worst luck best,
my first duty last;
He makes my sleepiest hour most euphoric,
my saddest moment least pathetic;
He makes me feel my own flesh under your skin;
He makes me feel thrilled as I have never been;
He makes seventh heaven and perdition not far;
He makes myself more primitive than you are.

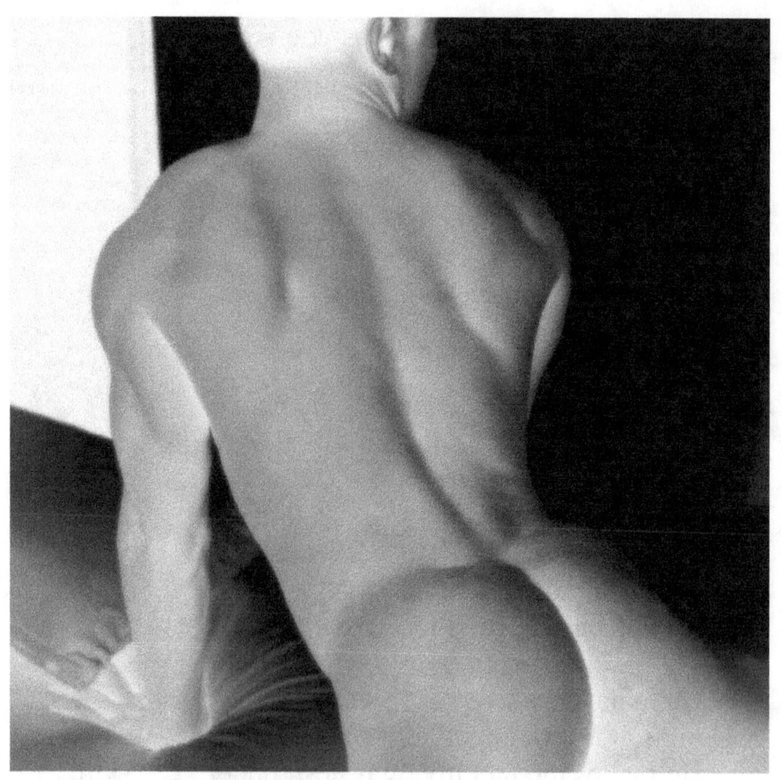

Insatiableness

I am oblivious to other things.
Things like the election, the train,
or a dying friend,
things that will function with
or without me and depend
on the immutable unchangeableness.

Sex with you is never amiss.
I have no concern
with you being a fugitive or a villain,
a dangerous criminal
with irrecusable status and power.
Conquer me as you please.

Colonise my body and enslave my spirit.
Irrigate the land that prays for rain.

Take all my money and throw it into the sea.
You offer me the pleasure for which I cannot pay.

For you everything is permitted.
Everything that inspires you
for brand new senses,
everything that keeps
your lips on mine intense.

This be the verse of my insatiableness.

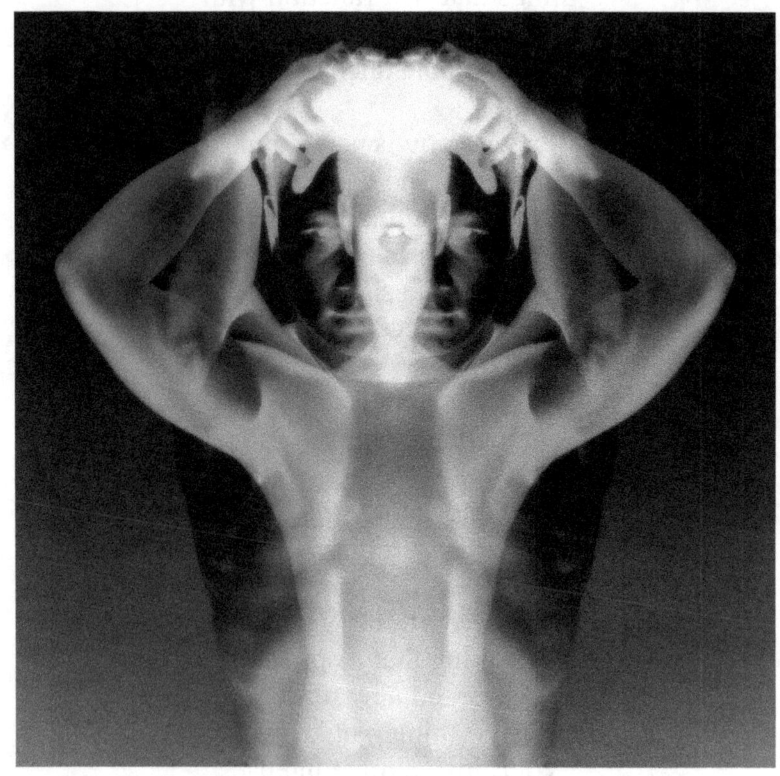

Beast With Two Backs

I am animal with you,
instinctive.

Years of education retreats into the black,
generations of evolution condenses into one act,
an act that always calls me back
to the open wild
where you and I are one
beast with two backs.

Life is brutally pleasurable.
My hair grows into yours
as the roots of a tree grip into the earth.
Our indefatigable energy
is the source of birth.

I stay animal for you,
appetitive.

I am a beast loyal to my hunger,
and you are my hunger of desire,
and I am your desire of thirst,
so suck me up with all your power.

Life is beastly enjoyable.
My core is nourished by your fire
that spits the cry of nature
that warms me up
and eventually makes me burn.

I am animal with you.
I stay animal for you.

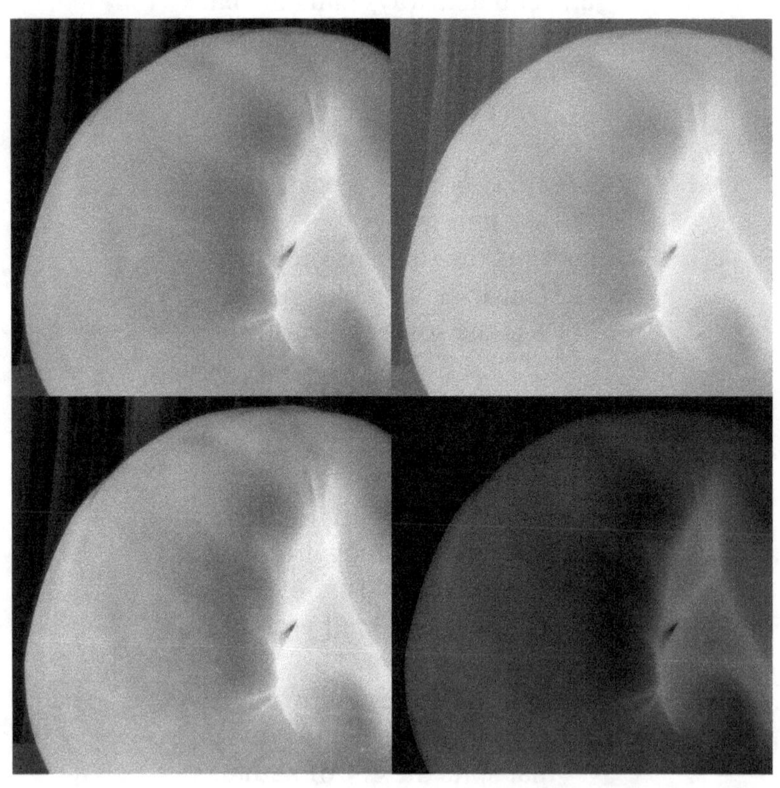

harvest

i have come to harvest your body,
the fatherland of my summer joy,
the fertile ground where pungent fruits grow.
i sweated, sunny days and rainy.

a godsend brings the golden season,
never mind anew my fondest toy,
never wonder despite the first snow.
a passion heats a fever crimson.

in due time the energy explodes,
then I return to a pampered boy,
then you turn into a barren mow.
in your eyes is the winter so cold.

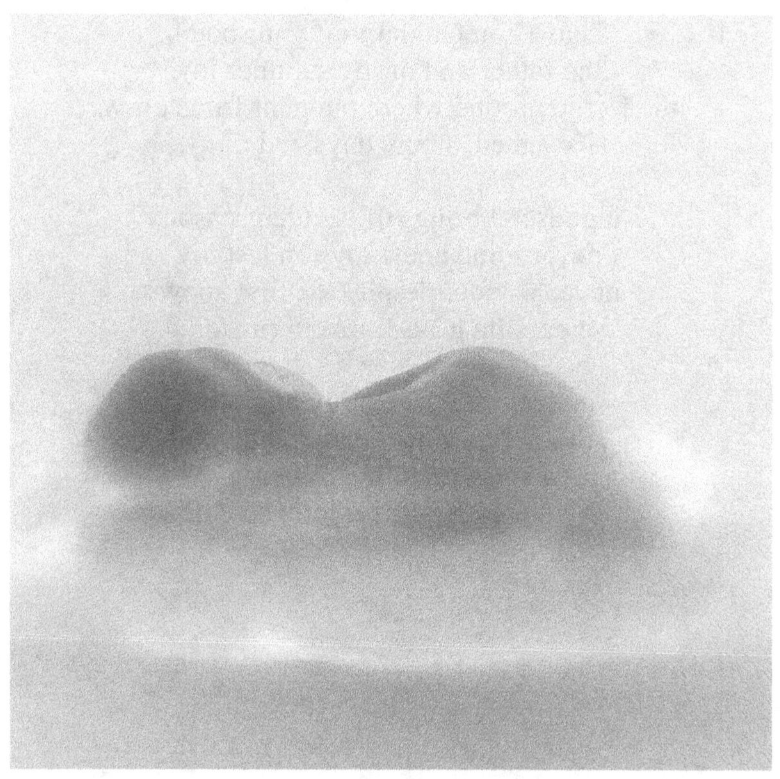

Winter And Three Other Seasons

Winter has finally withdrawn
consummating his long-overdue ejaculation.
It was the most intense rendezvous
I have never experienced with a nonhuman.
A celebrated orgy with countless orgasms
exhaust my vitality no sooner.
However, one wintry memory that I could thaw is
how my body was pushed to the extreme and
how I endured, meanwhile enjoying
the pleasure in pain.

Fully reloaded, he will return, claiming his owning.
But for now, I savour the foreplay with frigid spring
destined to grow ever more desirous
before the persuasion of high libido summer
in a blink of a leaf.
After all the sweat in passions of rain
and moans of crucial heat,
high spirit autumn
that was sung by Keats
will descend upon my scarlet bed.

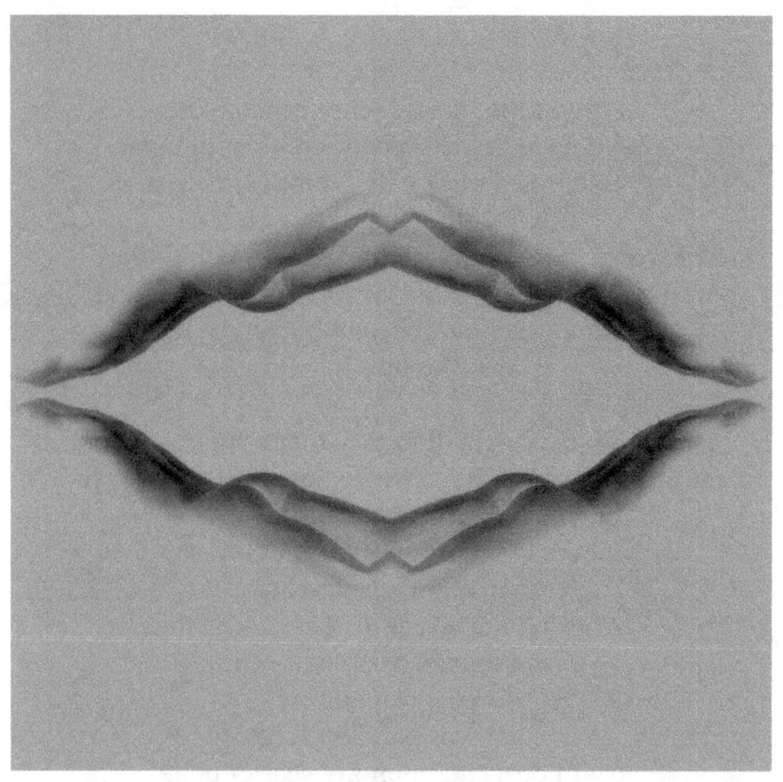

NEVER THE LESS

You are more distant than the dead
        will soon be forgotten,
        more immutable than the end
        is careless to return,
        more human than humanity
        has egos to defend,
        more unfair than the destiny
        decides who wins the best,

NEVER
THE
LESS,

I am more hopeful than a trust,
        more absolute than time,
        more personal than my black hole
        universal enough to lock you up inside.

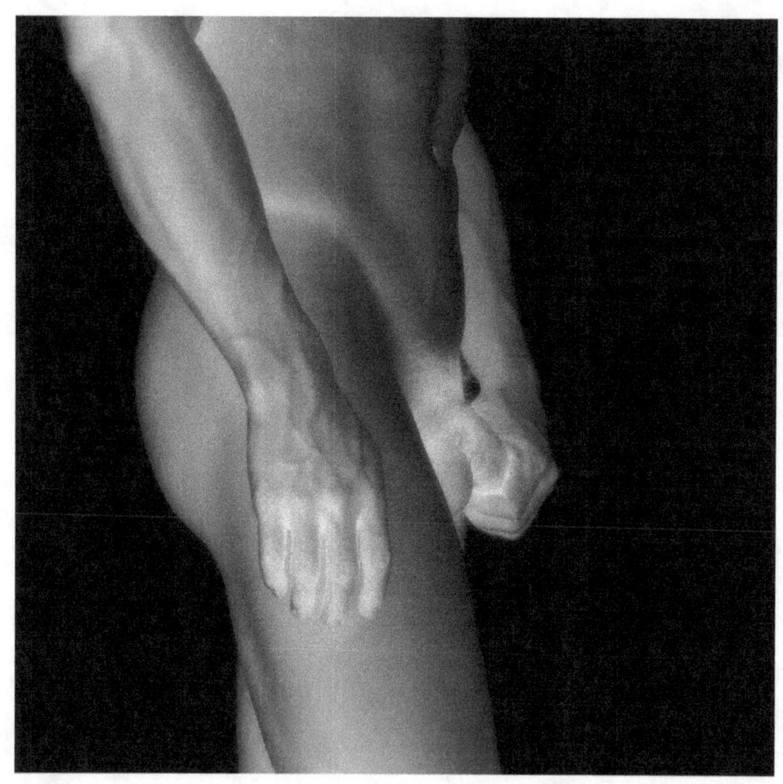

A Corporal Revolution

I am challenged by a corporal revolution
which strikes autonomously,
develops encouragingly,
and agitates my sensibility perpetually,
being invaded by your slightest approach.

But time will surpress it asexually,
itch after itch, quiver after quiver, urge after urge.

March by march, my body will

refuse to speak to your body of now heaven,
suppose we will not yet dwell in then hell,
in less than almost three short months;

shut down in the nearness of your body
opening up to every impossible kiss
in less than absolutely six full months;

scream the most strident horror over terror
in rememberance of your once so intimate body
in less than pathetic twelve long months.

Because my regime cannot be revolutionised
by Any Body, when time is unfairly on my side.

Happiness is a cheap emotion

Happiness is a cheap emotion

Happiness is a cheap emotion,
in its defense, still more than rare.
More than love that does not give,
more than beloved that cannot be given.

What about freedom? Is it a happy rival?
There is no free wisdom in my prison.
My kingdom is free from freedom.
You happy not be there.

Why do I hate in love but
remember outside of forget?
You are not alone not giving.
No one wants to be not there.

You are not there and I am not not here.
where are we both not staying?
Cry do we when why are we,
laugh in a rose but no freedom.

Excuse my love, excuse not freedom,
no free love is yes in my kingdom.
Seems to me not there I can go,
stay here I am but alone forget.

I am not free remember yet happy forget.
Same tonight after not same us forever.
One more kiss in one less night,
I stay where we are not happy in love.

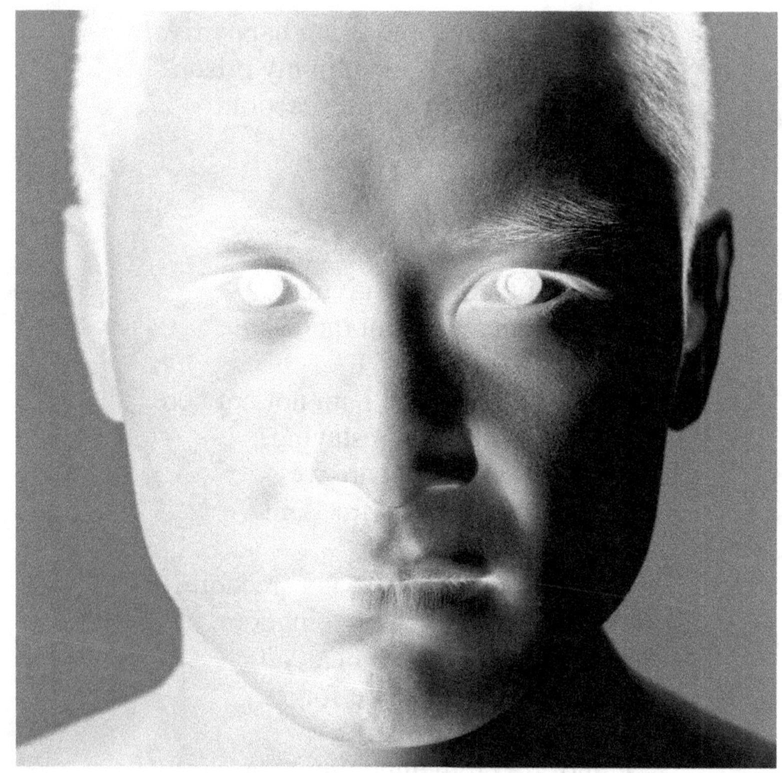

Rant After A Seperation

The scale of my emotion
is unmeasurable like an ocean.
The range of my passion
is as large as a mountain.
But I am master of
neither an ocean
nor a mountain,
and I cannot hinder an earthquake,
or prevent a volcano from eruption,
or deviate the route of the light year
that travels through saturn,
or collect the rain on a november night
and force the water
to flow back into the fountain,
or attempt to decipher
the undecipherable pattern
of my inner universe,
the ancient creation.

So gofuckyourself.

gigolo(the penis in my head)

gigolo(the penis in my head)

only true love cannot buy me
only fake hate may still try me
i live my own life without me
damn! losers, they do envy me

the penis in my head has its own will
never giving a fuck without a bill
never taking a shit from someone grown
my penis is rock-hard when fully blown

the price is higher than licking
some old, some dry or some black ass(puss)
the pain is nothing but fucking
fame and fortune then dropping seeds

the penis in my head is its own slave
craving much more when getting what it craves
droping sperm swarmed with meant to be losers
my penis deflates as a sham bruiser

THE cock is

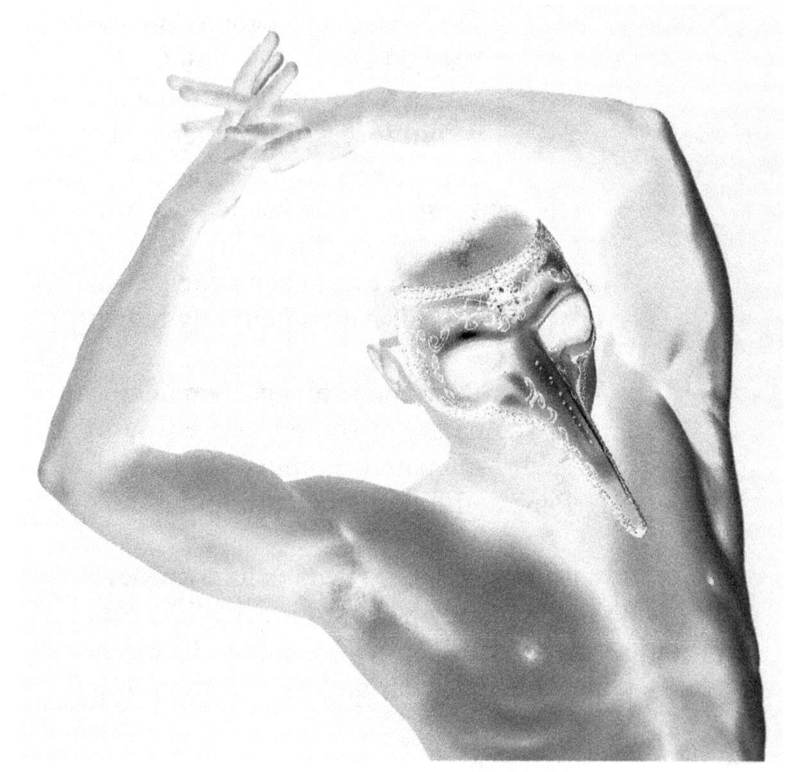

THE cock is

THE cock is
not any conquered earthquake
or any corner near a lake

THE cock is
not any cola licking luck
or any coffin in which i fuck

THE cock is
not any cop paid to puke
or any con nailing a nuke

THE cock is
not any cost caused by a strike
or any coward unlikely warlike

THE cock is
not any courting jerk
or any cobra being berserk

THE cock is
not any condom ditched by Dominick
or any comedian mouthing my dick

THE cock is
just any copy of a peacock

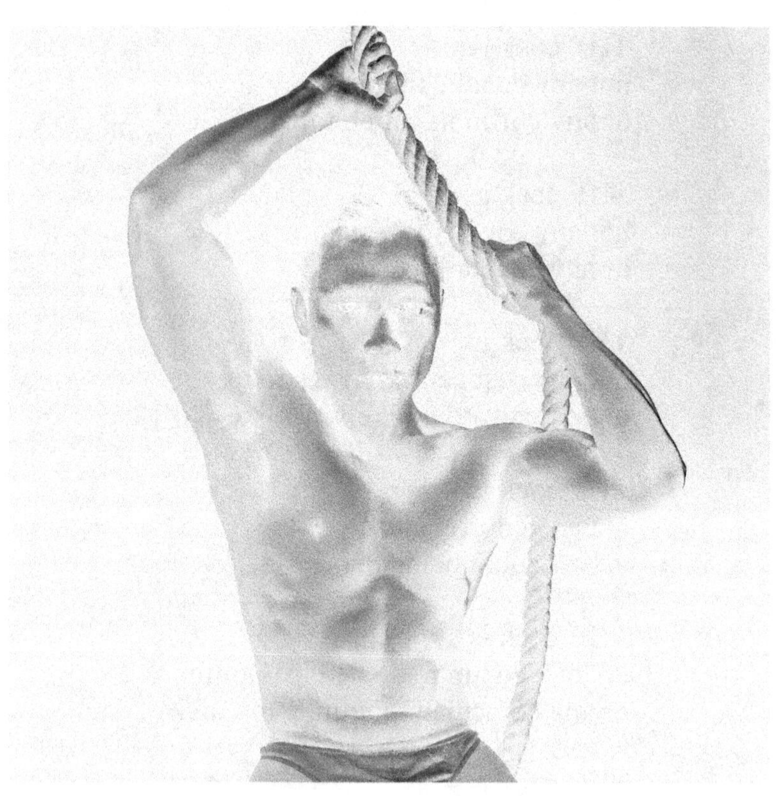

When I am the dictator

When I am the
                dictator
                        in a world of
ideologies,
I will a come plish an absolute genocide
against the race identified as
                                stupidity.

Since you are a
                diktaker
                        in the age of
decadence,
please cons you mate your operatic suicide
before the audience horny for a
                                farce.

I am a terrorist

I am a terrorist against myself.
I carry on mass destruction
against my peace of mind.
Embodied in me are a hundred religions
tearing me apart.
There is no justice to claim in my system.
Good and evil are one.
The villain and the victim are one.
The judgement is righteous.
This is my nature,
more than nurture.

I am a tyrannt against my existence.
I perpetrate the crime of genocide
against my confidence.
Buried in me is the immense hatred
refusing to be redeemed.
There is no salvation en route before the doom.
Lower and lower I sink.
A river of frenetic blood I bleed.
The prophecy is accurate.
This is my destiny,
this is my fate.

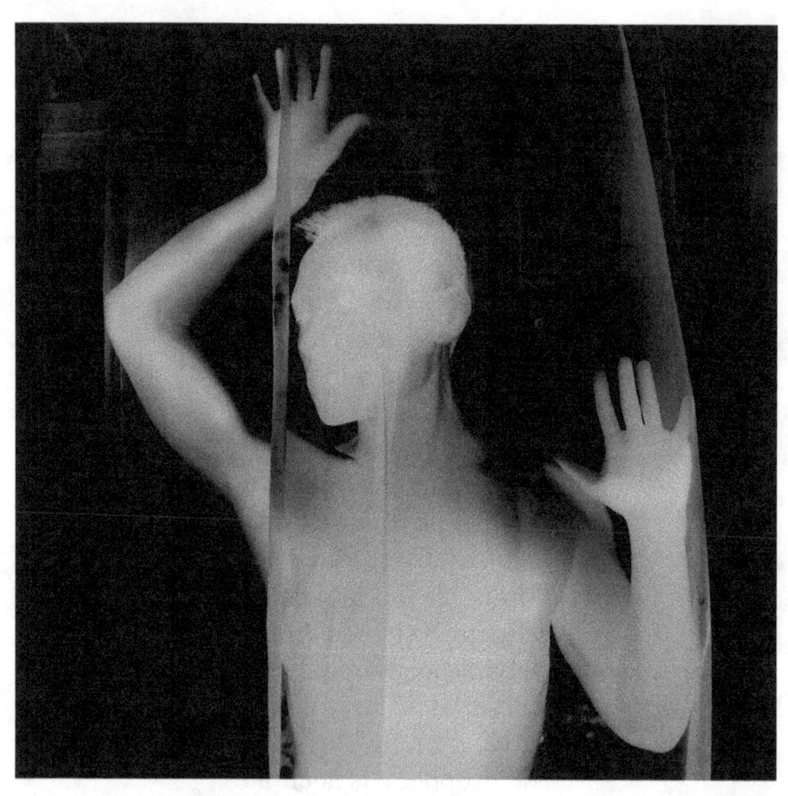

Hence

Hence

Infinitely small is infinitely
bigger than nothing at all.
                        Whatever
hopeless comparison a hopeful mind
may or may not conceive, yes maybe no
turns out to be forever the last hope.

Hence, before I have to indulge myself,
I endevour to indulge something else.

An immediate happening can be
sooner or later than now.
                        Whatever
unbelievable truth a believed lie
may or may not become, absolute if
holds the questions to the answers so few.

Hence, before I have to torture myself,
I find my way home in the cloud. Please help!

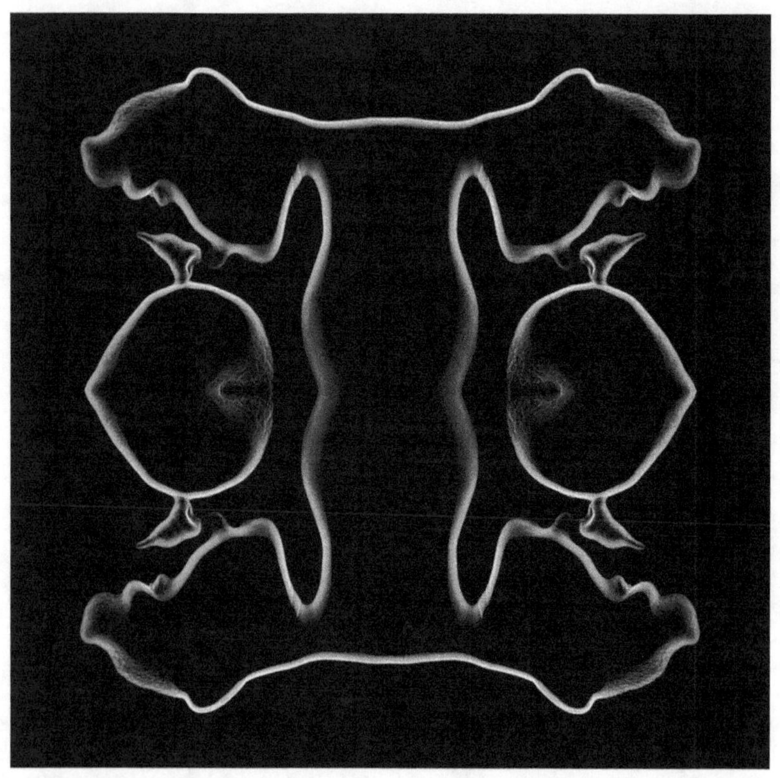

Life is the disease

Life is the disease whose patients
are heads with minds.
                        1, 2, 3, 4
thinkings dictate
                    5, 6
                        feelings,
7
   nuances give birth to
8
   nonsense,
                9
                    names fail to call
10
    personalities at once,

and
        every
                spring
                    is a
                        relapse.

Life is suffering

Life is suffering

Life is suffering,

and
yet
or
unless
hence/since/once
provided/so/in order that
whether/if/only if/as if/even if/(al)though
before/while/after/until/by the time
as long/much/soon as
how-/when-/wherever
more/less than
in case
lest
because

we are surviving.

This is becausewhy

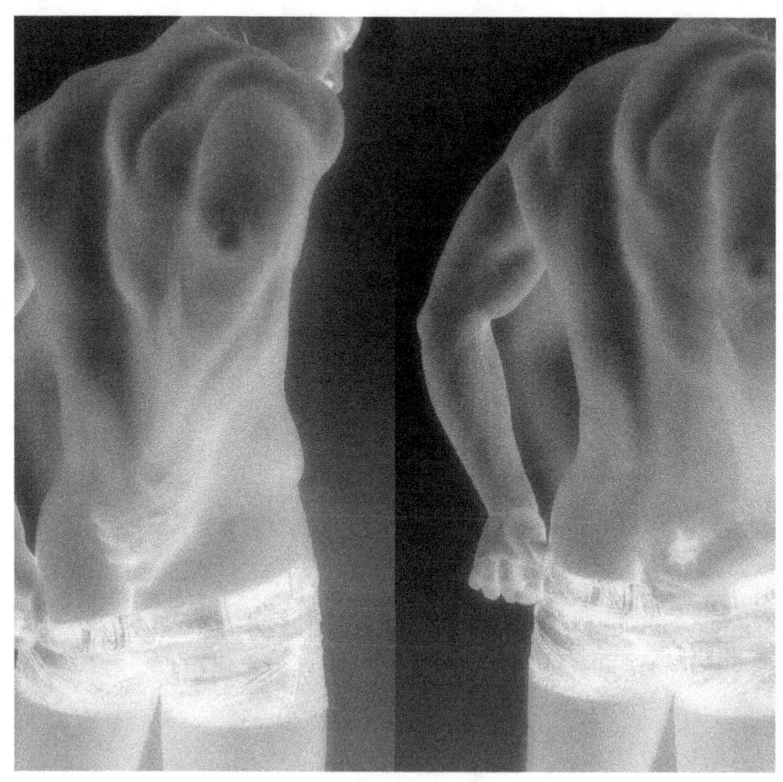

155

This is becausewhy

I am egocentrically bored
when
I am not the center of the world
where
I am eccentrically ignored.

This is becausewhy

I am eccentrically ignored
when
I am not the center of the world
where
I am egocentrically bored.

Pride!

Pride!

Pride!
My dearest foe, my closest kin.

You hurt me more than love could live,
you fool me more than hate could kill,
I feed you with my love and hate,
until you make me live to kill.

Pride!
My mind is weak, my heart grows rock.

Jealous fire is scorching hot,
I feel no more what is and not.
You bring me less gold but more shame,
a life without you bear I not.

To my idols

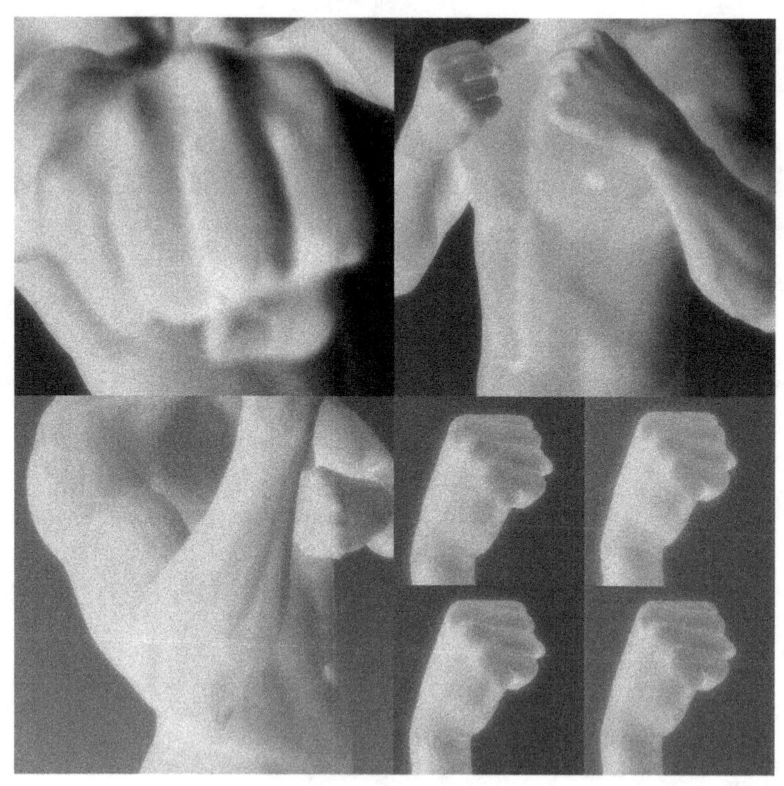

To my idols

The older you are, a proud monster
is becoming you. You are monstrous.
You deceive your forgotten belief
in a forever angelic self.

Was that beauty someone else's or
no one else's face was you being false?
How your voice sang sweeter than a bird
singing the ageless youth at its best!

Do you mourn the bird's death in the cage?
I do forgive your rage for old age.
And I do not nourish a monster
in my youthful ageing disaster.

As my pride never lets me transform
into whatever pride I am not.

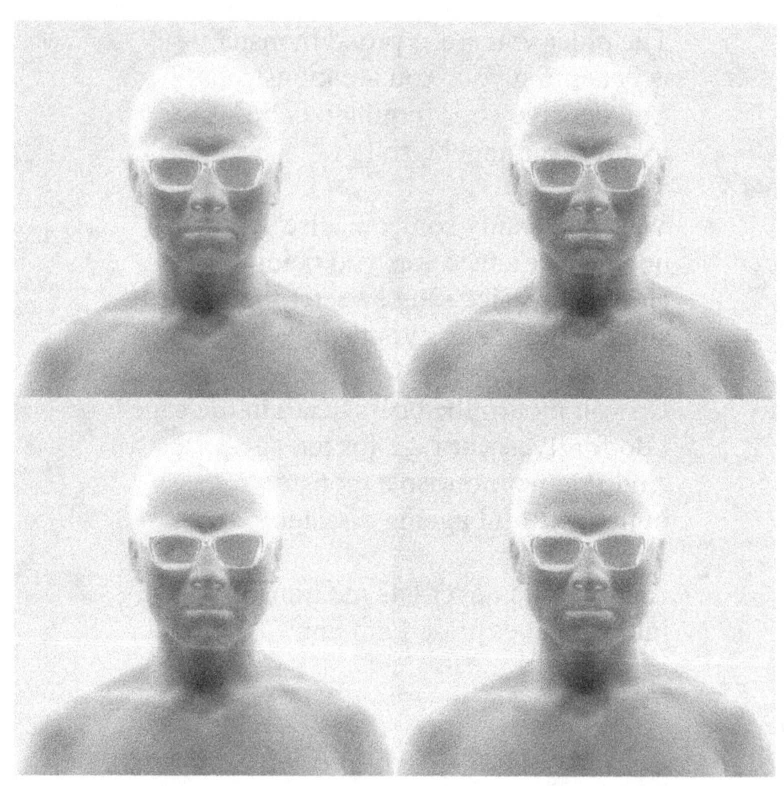

Godless

I need not whichever God to bless me,
his blessing will keep me from living free.
I touch, I can feel, I doubt, I am real,
I want not whatever mercy from him.

I am a lost cause, priests preach not at me.
I am proud, my spirit is wild and free.
I love life more than anybody else.
I am full of love, not because of him.

I envy not paradise. Excuse me,
how much is the ticket? Nothing is free.
And how many have lost their lives for hell?
Well, you must say, "nothing comes before him."

A holy book defines you, but not me.
Please believe in it, since you are not free.
I answer not to the futility,
something beyond all powers, even him.

albeit no

163

albeit no evil gods
there are still good devils
so let the door to hell stay wide open
when every window in heaven closes

albeit no common sense
there is still true falsehood
for a mind exists between right and wrong
when either side fears of absoluteness

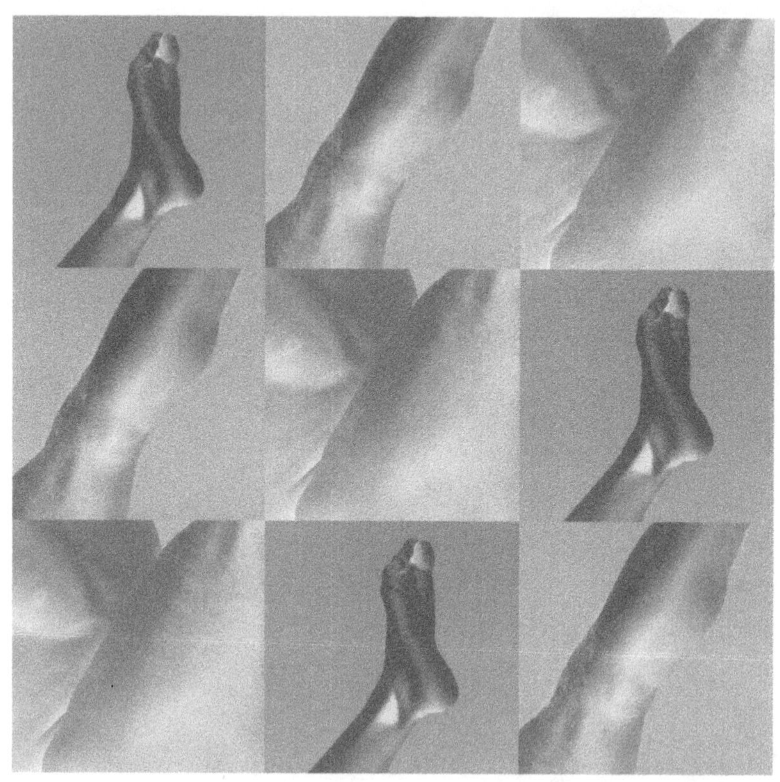

a rat and a cat

a sightless rat & a toothless cat
lose to find peace in each other's doom

nature's logic explains:
imperfection has its perfect match

the loveless she & the hateless he
find to lose doom in each other's peace

humans' nonsense complains:
a paradox owns its counterpart

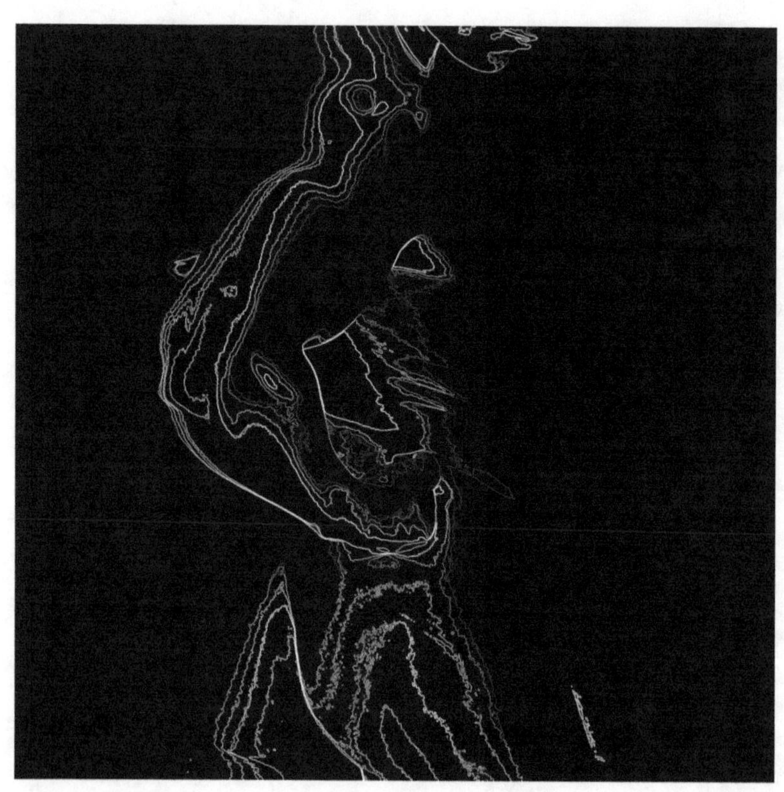

r u(of all adjectives) prau 2 b
a human,
a woman
or simply yet sophisticatedly
a man
sins u(of all adjectives) r prau 2 b
whatevercountry man
especially
patriotically
A MERI goroundrollingaround a trash CAN?

A Stone

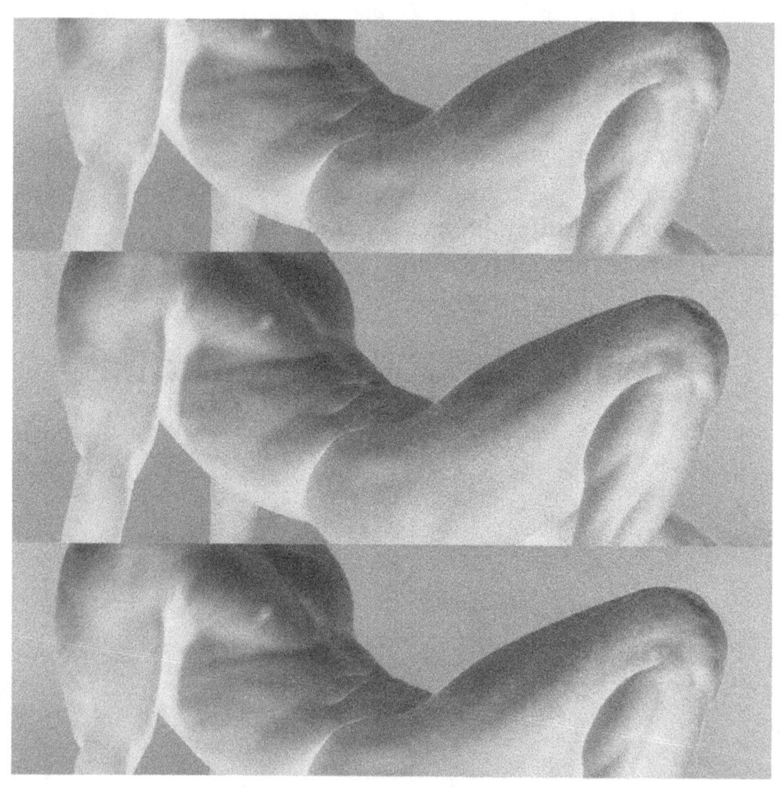

A Stone

I observe a stone that petrifies me. It used to be
a human that talked more than he could not walk.
It weights on the ground to soften back to mortal.

I kick it, it hurts me back no less. I grudge
my usual stony intensions that serve me no moral use.
I am the one who never learns to be mistreated gratis.

My foot starts to feel like it is someone else's.
It dehumanizes faster than the green of spring.
No one tries to cripple it as long as they breathe.

The sun shines unjudgingly on my past human life.
My heart of stone cries for the immobilised reason.
I miss a foot to kick me so that I can roll at least.

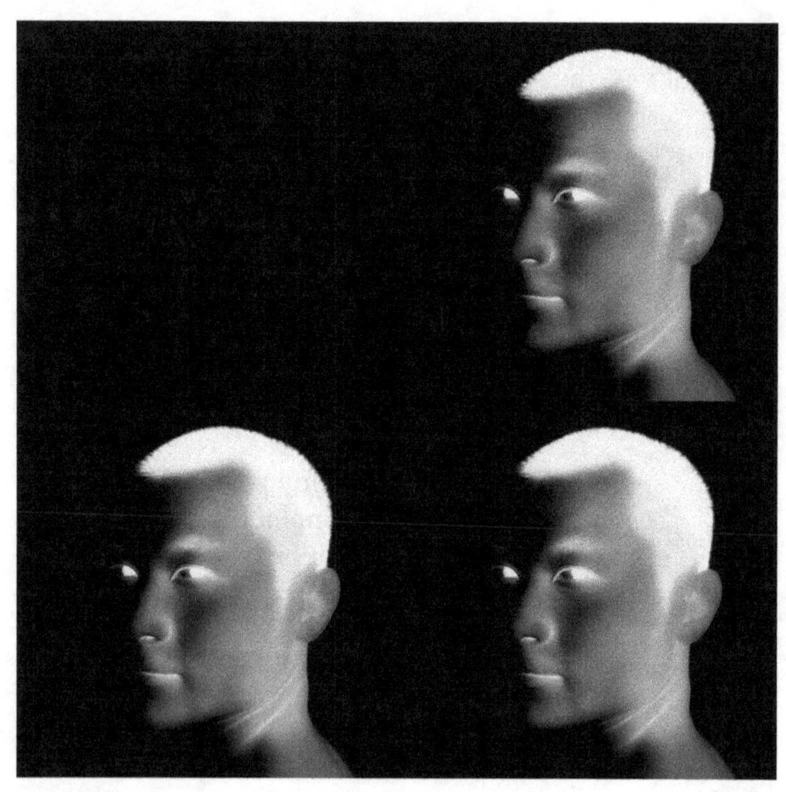

MONEY & POWER & FAME

MONEY & POWER create romance
for minds which often lose too much sleep
fantasising about even more
(poor & weak)ly created romance.

FAME appears romantic by itself
for eyes (seeing what wants to be seen)
and sounds the same as it smells and tastes
wherever anonymous selves feel.

should one not survive the other two,
just do as everyone does at home.
should all three suffice for a life time,
never let the romans rebuild rome.

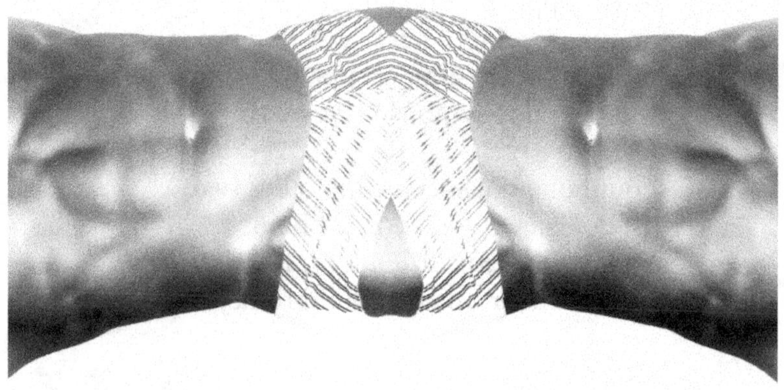

Rock N Roll vs. Ass N Holes

old was a time when Rock N Roll
new are bitches wet Ass N Holes

                    screaming hair hurt yet musical
                  rapping shit smells but whimsical

smart and dumb records were out sold
dumb and dumb digitals download

                     he broke a leg to suck a toe
                  she grinds to the beats monotone

a guitar in hand, new hero!
a plastic cheating hag, bravo!

                drugs to go, drag on with the show
                  money galore, burn it solo

life was fame, not unbearable
sex is shame but still fuckable

                nonsense raged like a thunderbolt
              bullshiters' moans could sink a boat

          long live hence Chopin concerto
        to silence dead all Rolls N Holes

Now hear me bore you

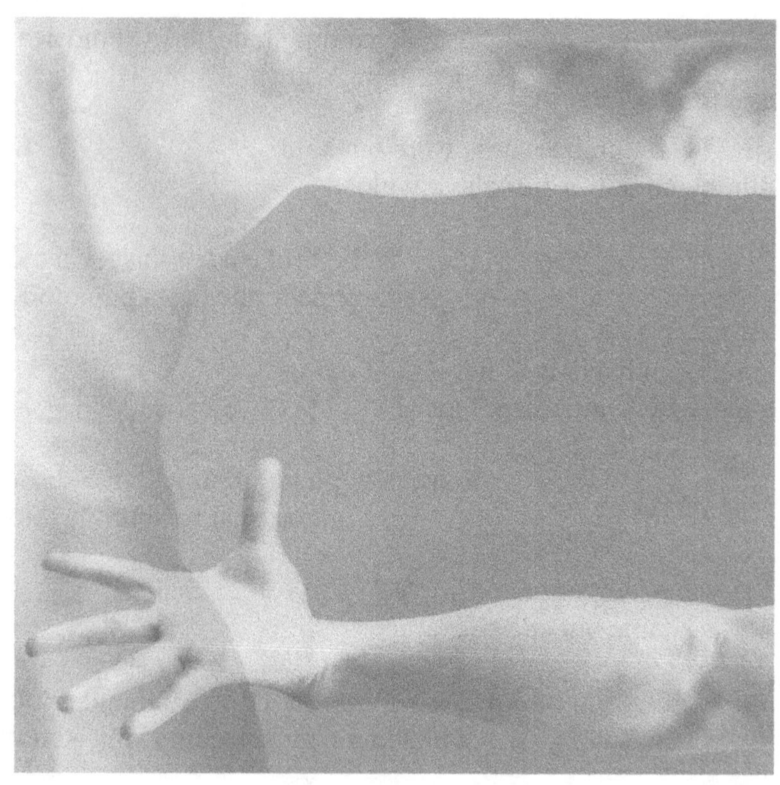

Now hear me bore you

now hear me bore you with my own stupid
love song that's just stupid enough to be
understood by those who are stupid in
love:
        yes, love me, love you, love is love, o...
why do you, why do i, why do we hate/hurt
each other? no one will ever know, no,
but we'll never forget until the end
of time for we'll remember forever.
trust me. always, i believe you, don't break
my heart, mi corazon, my dear, darling,
the sun and moon, stars, summer, sky, rain, snow,
eyes, dreams, every day and night, i miss/want you,
forgive me, one more chance, one and only,
can't live, don't leave, lonely, happy, crazy,
you make me feel, it's (not) too late, together,
you're mine, i'm yours, you take my breath away,
my boy, your girl, the most beautiful, it's true,
i'm dying, baby, baby, baby, please,
we don't say goodbye, so kiss me goodbye!

make your life a

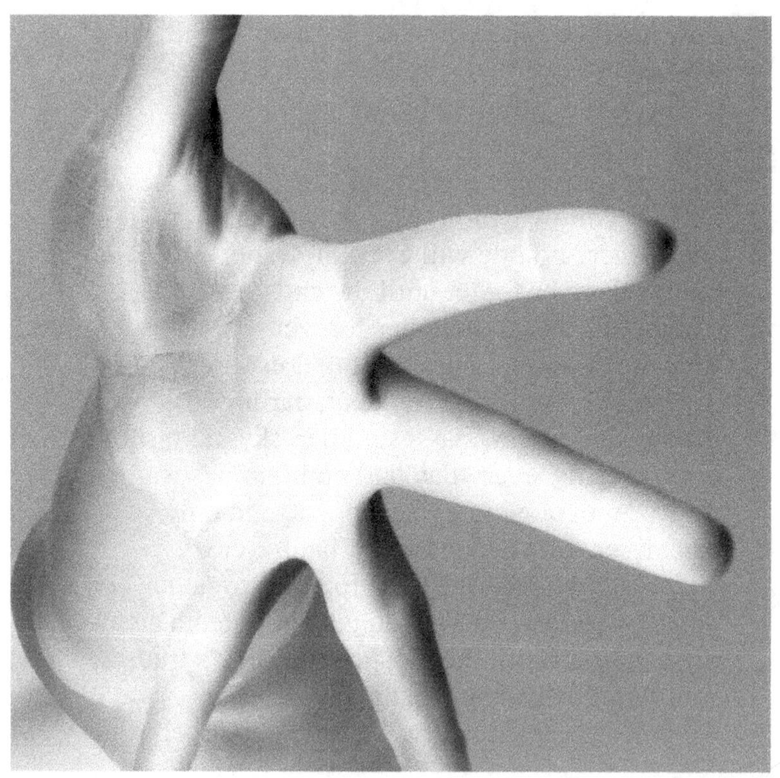

make your life a

failures seem
be-you-tiful
in ficKtions

hence,
write your life a ficKtion
:
twist and turn
till
mouth eats feet!

losers look
heroi(n-n)c
in muBis

hence,
shoot your life a muBi
:
fight and fall
till
break a neck!

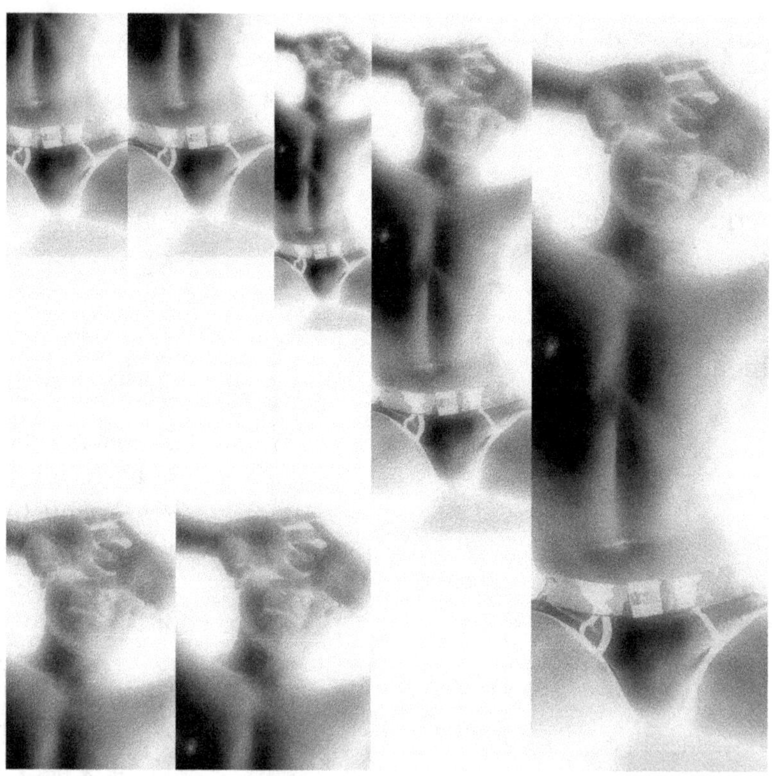

since in real life

since in real life, anyone could get killed,
let's go to the cinema and get fooled.
who cares if cinema sees the real life
as a perfect tale where someone gets loved?

someone. but we're already perfect fools
in real life, though none of us have got killed.

as long as none of us have got loved,
cinema is more real than the real life.

why does one love to get loved in real life?

to make cinema get killed like a fool.

in a perfect life, does a fool get killed?

nothing is perfect when no one gets loved.

My love is dirty, my hate, pure

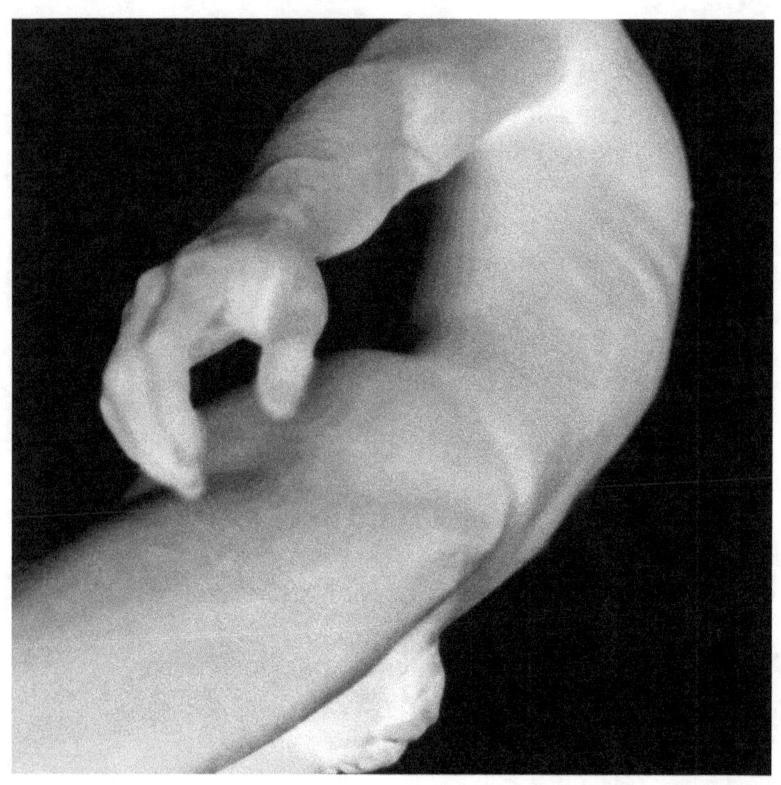

My love is dirty, my hate, pure

My love is dirty, my hate, pure;
my other craziness is lost
in translation from mind to soul.
And
my body feels without a cause.

My days are dreamy, my nights, wild;
my youth is a sleeping beauty
that ages despite my closed eyes.
And
my life escapes reality.

My good is real, my bad, too;
my good and bad shall make and break
all or nothing before too long.
And
my human nature is my sake.

what else?

183

what else?

what else is most
                boring than
a thing called style
                when
nothing else is most
                exciting than
faking a so-called artist?

what else is most
                hopeless than
two lovers fell in hate
                when
nothing else is most
                harmless than
a family trapped in a marriage?

what else is most
                forgivable than
reoccuring war and peace
                when
nothing else is most
                fuckable than
everybody's own happiness?

I HAPPENING TO BE HUMAN.

I must be loved

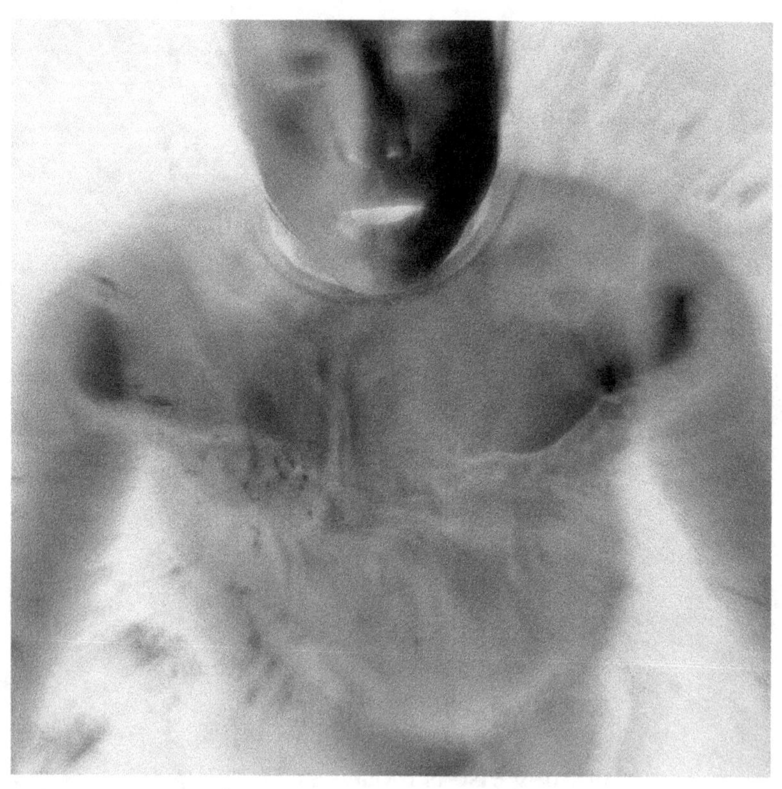

I must be loved

I must be loved, for there are too many
reasons to appreciate a flower
(rueing itself).
                Should beauty fail to be
appreciated, a flower may still
pick itself. To kill is at times to love.

I must be loved, for there are even more
reasons to misunderstand a dream world
(making itself).
                Till every dream comes true,
I would rather the world kept on sleeping.
A real world ever misunderstands love.

I must be loved, for there is not any
reason.

I am punished

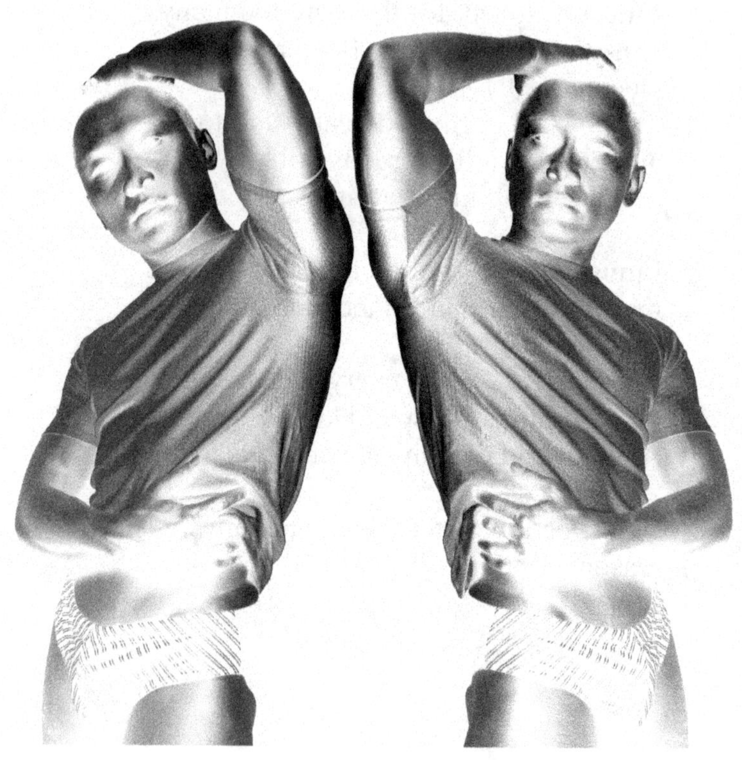

I am punished

I am punished in every personal
way:

     drowned in a dream drying on its ve
ry own importance,
               hanged high enough to
forget the weight of the ground,
                       burnt beyond
re cognition from a firy ego,

fooled by the music
               e
             c
           h
          o
            ing someone
else's pride and joy, (I am punisha
bly the beauty that I do not become),
bored by the perfection aiming at all

notions,
       (I concede the most imperfect
season in which my teeth rot, my eyes blur,
my sex refuses power less ly and
my soul punishes other souls being

un punished),
            wasted by the time(jealous
ly it favours death over youth) after.

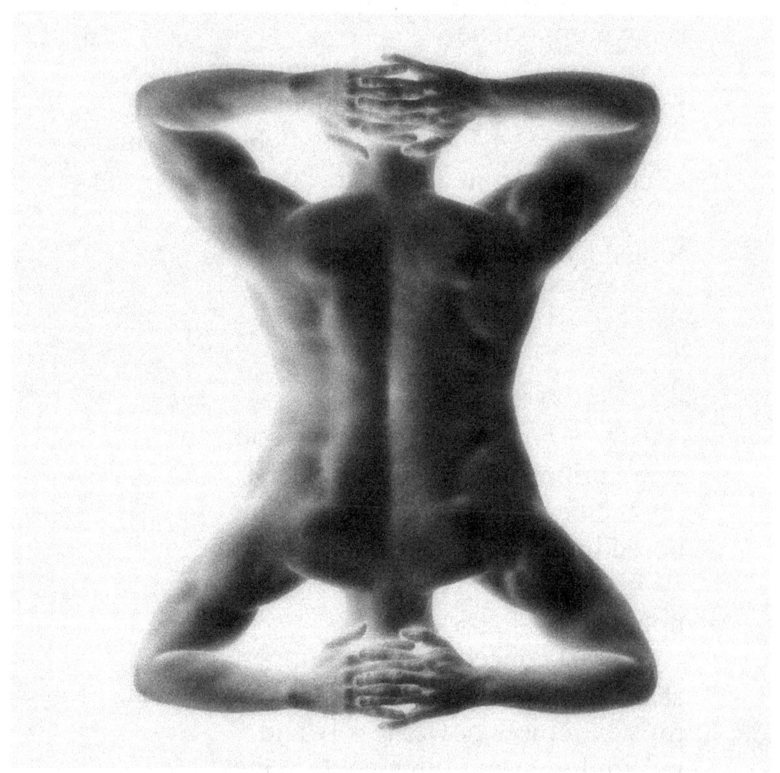

If living was less of a battle

If living was less of a battle

If
living was less of a battle than dying was most certain
and
loving deceived more than hating seemed least candid,
let
wanting deny nothing while needing admits all.

If
a body could be emptied into a desire
and
a key without a lock could be lost anyhow,
let
a truth mean no truth for a man who never seeks.

If
because forgot why everytime there comes the end
and
away unmeasurably pushed near untill now,
let
both first and last have faith in neither best or worst.

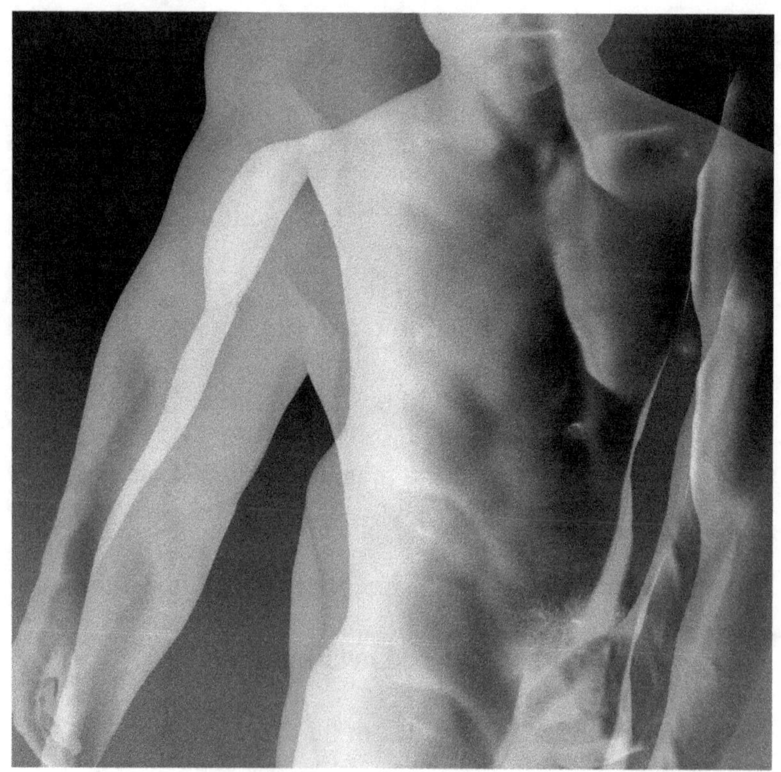

Sweet dreams dream of themselves

Sweet dreams dream of themselves

Sweet dreams dream of themselves
                              (better
than life does anything else) as
nightmares favor days over nights
(better than death does nothing else,
regardless of the heart chosen
for love to love itself truly).

Love loves itself uselessly
                           (if
realities remain unreal
for those who can but deem
both sweet dreams and nightmares real) if
hate hates itself naturally
(and everything else usefully).

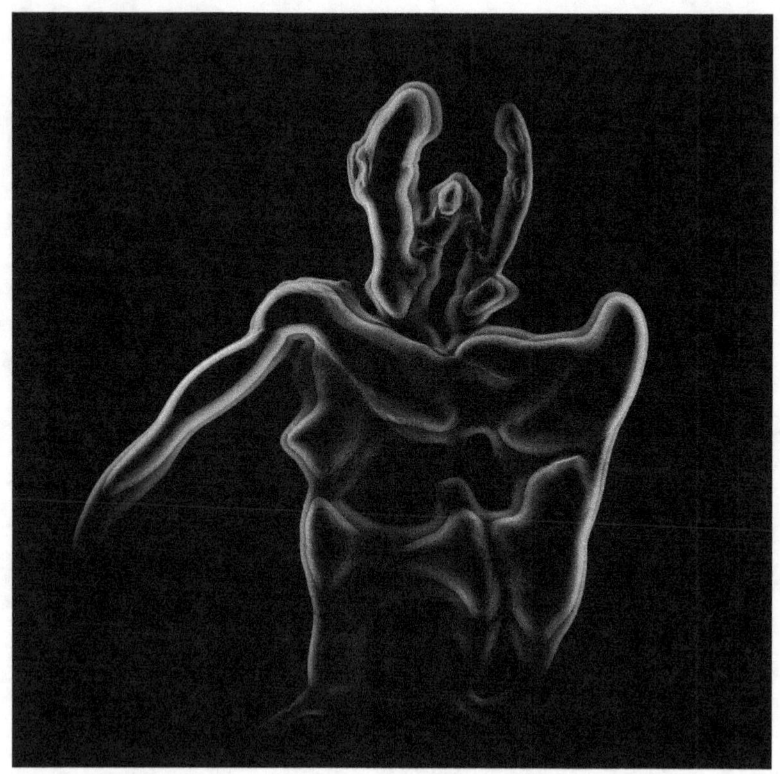

Two whos
lost their way to
somewhere over the rainbow

following

three whos
claiming to have
found the way to
somewhere else beyond the rainbow,

while

who is not hoping
somewhere under the rainbow. (?)

Death is the most

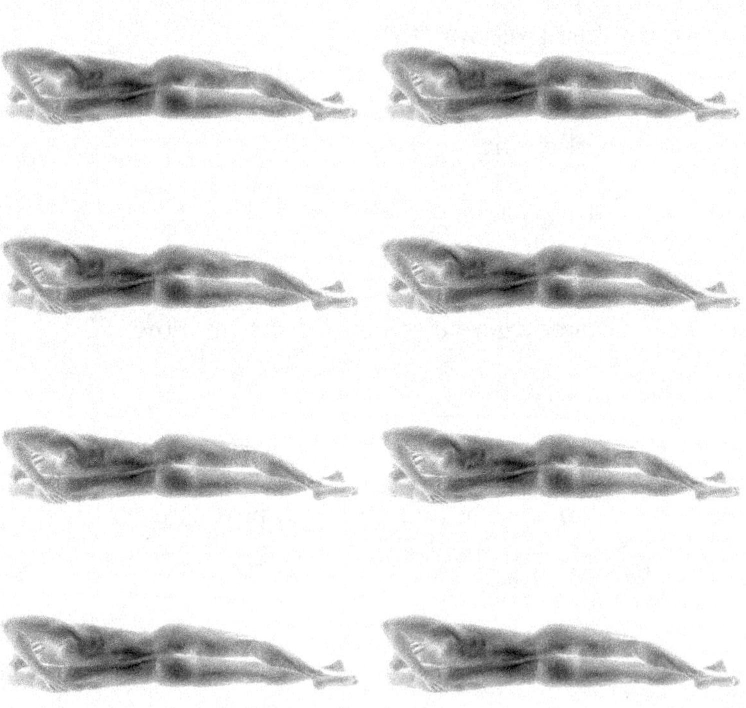

Death is the most

Death is the most (un)certain
amidst (un)certainties of life.

Or perhaps the least, but not last.

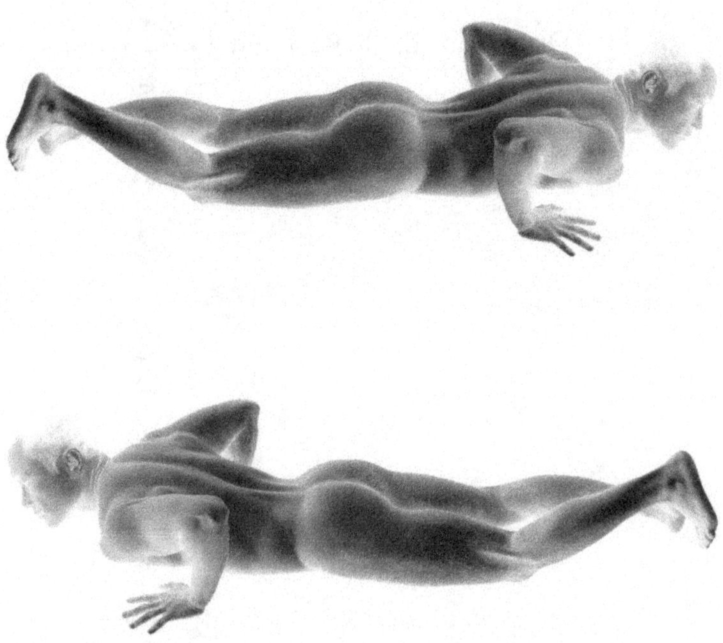

dreamless people; dreamful cities

dreamless people must be fearless of death,
careless of life, heartless and thoughtless of
the known and the unknown inside out, while,
nevertheless, doubtlessly meaningless.

dreamful cities must be fearful of days,
careful of nights, heartful and thoughtful of
the loved and the unloved through and through, while,
nevertheless, doubtfully meaningful.

the sun burns

the sun burns in the wind,
burns in the mind,
and burns in everything
of the absolute kind,
until
        nothing
                matters
                        to
space or time.

INDEX OF TITLES